Why marriages fail before the wedding?

Ingeniously designing the marriage you've always wanted.

By Walter Murandu

Copyright © 2023 by Walter Murandu

First edition, June 2023

Editors: Mukudzei Makumbinde, Rutendo Makumbinde & Felisters Makumbinde.

Cover designs: Caleb Bentil

Acknowledgements

I am deeply indebted to Pastor Mtho Gwebu, who has taught me many things I know today. Thank you sir, for your leadership and guidance to me and my family. Your words of encouragement are not in vain, and this book is proof of that.

I express sincere appreciation to all the couples I have walked with on their premarital counselling journey. More so, the couples I counselled until 2021, you all believed in my humble beginnings and my prayer for you is a long life, health, and a blissful marriage.

Dedication

This is the first of many books I intend to write. I am dedicating this book to my best friend and wife, Darlane. My wife, you have been nothing but the best and thank you for all your support, encouragement, and wisdom-filled ideas. You make it all worth the effort.

Table of Contents

Introduction

You desire to have a happy marriage. What would you do if the marital future of your dreams seems gloomy? Many newlyweds more and more appear to struggle or are caught up in a dilemma or are quitting marriage, even as their wedding ceremony recollections are nonetheless fresh. When everything you hoped for in marriage seems to drift far away before you even get hold of it. How do you stay hopeful in this era where many have lost hope in love and marriage?

You desired marriage from childhood. Perhaps we had a similar childhood, and you also liked the idea of marriage from a tender age. With my childhood friends, I used to role-play as a married father, and this is when the idea of marriage was born. With maturity, you have seen the good and the bad of love and marriage. You are wondering if your marriage dream will come true or if it's a fading fairy tale.

Perhaps you've been through a divorce, or you witnessed a divorce, or you grew up with divorced parents. Maybe your friend or relative lately confided in you about their marital troubles. Is there hope for you in marriage? Will your testimony be any different? Have you wondered before if divorce is inevitable? How do you hold on to the happy marriage dream after your glorious wedding day in such perilous times? How do you navigate your love journey to marriage and life after vows when it seems many are being hit on the blind-side in marriage?

You are not alone, and your situation is far from hopeless. There is nothing new under the sun. As far as humans are concerned, there is no other relationship that has survived time, evolution, industrialisation, globalisation, tokenization, and other forces of change, like marriage. Encourage yourself, let faith, hope, and love be your strength. Greater is the potential within you than the challenges you have experienced, seen or heard of in this world.

We live in an era where bad things virally spread, whilst the good and pleasant things of life and marriage go unnoticed. Your situation and experiences are not all there is to marriage. Millions of couples are enjoying blissful marriages every day and you may never learn about them because such stories don't sell. How many divorce headlines have you seen in newspapers and magazines? Divorce claims the first page while you may never read of any couple having a great marriage in such media.

Indulge my wisdom in the following chapters, and I will teach you how I have coached couples intending to get married to design the marriage they have always wanted. I am yet to receive a call from any of the couples I worked with reporting a serious marital problem. However, I am used to words of appreciation, happy marriage moments stories, and referrals for their friends and relatives to gain the same wisdom.

What you will learn in this book may not be a surprise to you. However, you will learn to recognise the foundational elements of marriage that are currently being trivialised, side-lined, and replaced. You will set your priorities right to prepare for marriage. Your status quo is about to be challenged by truth undiluted. Take your mind and heart for a roller-coaster ride as you discover what truly makes marriage seamless. You will not only be challenged, but deeply enriched in your understanding of love, relationships, and marriage through this book.

Understanding is key to application; an expert is simply a person who fully understands a particular subject. When you gain understanding, you will become an expert in your love relationship. When you have a thorough understanding of love, marriage, and your spouse, your dream of a happy marriage will become a reality. You owe marital success to yourself. You have no capacity to err expensively in your love life, no opportunity to cause remorse. Let us explore the hard truth of love matters together. I am expecting to receive your feedback at the end of the book.

Part A

Top six relationship deceptions in the 21st century

Part A

Introduction

Dressed in simple jeans, a t-shirt, flip-flops, scruffy hairstyle, and temporary tattoo stickers, an undercover cop disguised himself as a customer and gained the trust of a street drug peddler. In the excitement of striking a new customer, the peddler handed the undercover cop a stash of nose candy and accepted cash. The cop flashed his badge with the words, "you are under arrest". Stunningly surprised and failing to escape the scene, he sadly regretted falling for the deception.

Mr. undercover cop sold him a lie which he bought. The cop misled him to see a customer instead of his true self and intent. The cop could hide the truth and promoted a disguised image of himself to the drug dealer until it was too late. Such is deception, the victim is unaware until it is too late. Deception hurts the deceived. You may think you are in control, while you are not.

I have heard and seen many stories of people deceived or defrauded into losing enormous sums of money in romance scams, property scams, online scams, and many other types of fraud. Fraud is only possible under deceptive circumstances. Fraud is based on deception. Whoever deceives you has defrauded you of something to your detriment or to their gain.

Indeed, there is an increase in deceptive relationship scandals coming to light on social media. People deceive each other in relationships, but the deception I will discuss in this book is macro deception, deception on a national and global scale. The type of deception that exists in romantic relationships' knowledge pot. The deception that a wrong or twisted truth can become a norm and is acceptable in society. I am convinced that such weak knowledge or solutions in relationships have led to the rise of breakups and divorce, which is the ultimate of a failed relationship.

There are common beliefs and behaviours in romantic relationships that people engage in, thinking it is beneficial for their relationships and only to realise (usually too late), they have created a troubled future. A troubled future, just like the drug peddler who sold illegal drugs to an undercover cop. With ease of access to media channels globally, we have witnessed entertainment being prioritised at the cost of culture and good morals. The information you hear and what you see shapes your thoughts and imagination, which translates to your reality in time. What you hear and see about relationships and marriage can grow into your real-life experiences. Whoever informs you, feeds you, and you can't outgrow the quality of your feed.

From Generation X, Millennials to Generation Z, most people spend a considerable amount of their time on social media. The Internet of things has enabled many to create or consume online content with ease. This, compared to the past, where only beneficial, credible and verifiable sources could create content, has led to almost anything being publicised and going viral. What you hear or know about marriage shapes your marital destiny. It is your sole responsibility to consume content from sources that build you up and prepare you for the marriage you desire.

One sad deception growing in popularity is movie scenes of how a married couple has sex out of duty, while inundated with house chores, children, and boredom. This is contrasted to first dates, who on the same night have a steamy sex session in the car or anywhere in their apartment. On their way to bed, they tear each other's clothes, throw shoes and wallets anywhere, kiss every erogenous zone, and make explicit sexual sounds like it's the highlight of their lives.

Of course, it's a movie. In real life, we know we will need to wear the clothes again, and so we do not tear clothes for sex. They portray uncommitted relationships as acceptable, fun, robust, adventurous, and spontaneous, while portraying marriage as the terminator of any opportunity for sexual delights, and freedom of choice or movement.

King Solomon in the book of proverbs said, "as a man thinketh in his heart, so is he", your heart is your subconscious mind. Media speaks directly to your subconscious mind and any ideas you do not reject consciously will soon become your own. In other words, you become what you watch and surround yourself with.

No wonder why many young adults are hesitant and delaying marriage. Preferring sex with no commitment, all because of the information they are being exposed to. Marriage is not boring, and the romance shown in movies is an act produced by paid professionals working from a script, not a reality. After watching many scenes like this, one's mind cannot help differentiating reality from a professional entertainment act. Owing to such exposure, we now have many young adults fear marriage may make them weary and fall out of love. Young adults who should be married by now are still asking questions like why get married to divorce? I must first enjoy and explore my youth. Why rush to marry?

This is an error under the sun, an epidemic of young people who are not marrying or delaying marriage yet competing with married people on sex knowledge, frequency, and styles. In contrast, those who desire to marry are clueless about how to prepare for marriage, let alone how to sustain a happy union. This phenomenon negatively affects the institution of marriage and the fruits thereof. Anything you don't prepare for and train for sets you up for a shocking failure.

My niece desired to be an actuarial scientist. She would have to undergo years of university studies and incur enormous costs before she can practise actuarial science successfully in the industry. A distinguished career requires significant time and financial investments. So does a distinguished marriage. Before you practise in marriage, you must pay the price and gain knowledge by time spent learning about marriage, and how to be an excellent husband or wife.

As I inquired about purchasing a gun for self-defence in November 2021, I realised the cost was not an issue, but applying for a gun licence meant I would have to go through training, conduct behaviour assessments, and undergo a criminal record check. Although I wanted the gun, the licence was a prerequisite. Imagine if I had bought the gun with no training? I'd be a danger to society. The same is like having untrained love birds on the altar. It won't take them long before they hurt each other and those around them, and sometimes the risk is fatal.

In order to get my driver's licence, I had to learn the road rules and regulations and pass an exam with a score of 90% or higher. Anything less would be a failing grade, thus incompetence to drive on public roads. Following the test, I had to do a road driving test with an inspector scrutinising my parking and driving ability.

To be adept at anything that is financially beneficial, one must educate themselves, get tutelage, and pass an evaluation before using their skills. Think of a situation where you walk into a hospital and the practising staff says he or she has not been to medical school but has confidence that they can perform your friend's heart surgery. What would you do? My guess is you would sue the hospital for having untrained staff practising medicine and report this fellow. Marriage is not the place for untrained yet practising heart surgeons. An untrained spouse has a strong propensity to produce broken and bruised hearts.

If you order a ride-share service and the driver is a 13-year-old, would you take the ride? As a teen, they would have no right to operate any vehicle, let alone public transportation, so he would have to be reported to the authorities. If there is a driver like that behind the wheel, you will get to heaven before time. The driver is a danger to themselves, their passengers, and the community at large. How can it be that some married people haven't developed past the maturity of a 13-year-old? We should not give such people a marriage licence. If your fiancé is this underdeveloped, refuse to be their passenger until they mature in marriage matters.

If you cannot be a driver without training, a medical doctor without training, a gun owner without training, then we should also not permit people to marry without training. It is quite unfortunate that this is not part of our government authorities' concern to make sure consenting adults are competent to build a successful marriage. The authorities simply issue a marriage licence to anyone who has a witness without checking if this person or couple has gone through training or exhibiting competence in marriage matters.

A community comes from families and families from marriages. Bringing babies into the world and raising them is best done within the context of marriage. It is perilous to have an untrained and unlicensed person in the driver's seat. The institution of marriage is critical to society and a powerful tool, just like a gun. In the hands of an untrained person or couple, the gun becomes a danger to themselves and everyone in the vicinity.

If you have struggled in your past relationships, failed to grow a relationship into marriage, seen a marriage that is boring and starved of joy, peace, and happiness, or think your marriage may end in tears. Worry not, this book is designed not only to give you hope, but to take you through a path that leads to marital bliss.

My mentor always says, "there is no mountain anywhere, the only mountain in your life is your ignorance". In my few years of relationship counselling and coaching, I have found this to be a plausible fact if applied to marriage. Wisdom in how to have a happy and problem free marriage does not come from age but is a product of acquired and practised wisdom, not assumed knowledge. I have seen old but foolish behaving people in marriage.

Many individuals and couples assume they know it all about the marriage they intend to start. An assumption is the mother of all failures. Premarital counselling is learning how to drive the marriage car safely before you find yourself behind the wheel. Learning to drive a car costs far less than the cost of a car accident. The cost to learn how to co-drive your marriage can not compare to the cost of marital accidents, the cost of a toxic marriage and divorce.

Lack of training is the principal cause of gun accidents. Gun proficiency training lessons cost nothing compared to the costs of unintended death, injury, medical bills, pain, loss of work time and permanent health problems.

Take a pose and reflect on your own life. Anything that you do well is something you have invested time to learn. You can run or jog without falling because you spent a better part of your first four years of your infancy learning how to trigger muscle movement, move your legs, crawl, stand, walk, and finally running and even better to run while dribbling a ball. This ability did not just appear from the blue but is a product of a lengthy step by step learning process and so is the institution of marriage.

In the following chapters, you will learn a truth that is no longer popular but is pivotal to your marital success. You will understand why you may need to postpone the wedding to allow time to prepare adequately for marriage? Why you need premarital counselling, when to start and finish premarital counselling, how to choose a good counsellor, etc…

My marriage has enjoyed marital bliss from the altar, today and forever will because of the truth I have taken time to put together in this book. If my wife and I could do it for one week, one month and one year, then I am convinced we can repeat the same for 50 years and till death do us part. Wisdom is repeating the same winning formula and winning each time, while stupidity is doing the same foolish thing, expecting a different result.

In Part A of this book, I will explore six strong deceptions that have led to many failed relationships and marriages. The one who teaches and informs you can control you. Today, we have un-informed information floating everywhere on social media. Being deceived or lied to means someone or something made you to believe a wrong thing to be correct or correct thing as wrong. It is easy to fall for a deception, but staying in it is a choice. Only the truth can set you free from deception, and I wrote this book to promote your knowledge of truth.

Chapter 1

Love is all you need.

Love is all you need. If you love each other, you will be happy in marriage. Love is blind. I have heard these statements repeatedly in many circles of information exchange and they can be misleading. The statements have led to masses of people seeking after love only and consciously or unconsciously ignoring other critical pillars that make love stand the taste of time.

The most selling books across all genres are romance novels, the most selling movies are romance movies, the same is true for songs, love songs are more appealing to people across all races, gender, culture, ages, and social affiliations. There is nothing wrong with celebrating and encouraging love. We celebrate love across all nations, cultures, races, and generations, which alludes to everyone's innate desire to give love and receive love.

Many define love as an emotional feeling of excitement about someone or a spark. Love is not a feeling, but feelings can express the love you already have. If love was just a feeling, you would not desire it as you have learned from your personal experience, that feelings are unreliable, constantly, and quickly change. Feelings are just feelings, and they will be nothing more in a relationship or marriage. Love must be something more than just dopamine, oxytocin, serotonin, and endorphin brain chemicals.

Imagine being in a relationship with someone whose love is as strong as their moods, feelings, or emotions. In real terms, you are single as a pringle, just waiting for the day you will be dumped. True love has no feelings but is a choice. Love starts with a decision, a decision to love someone. I honour the work and life of Dr Myles Munroe of blessed memory. In his definition of love, there is nothing to add or subtract. He said, "love is a decision to meet someone's needs for a lifetime expecting nothing in return".

Love is not mysterious, but lust, infatuation, and confusion are. Love is an important decision you make. You must decide to love someone. It is a choice. This understanding eliminates the notion of "falling in love" as you consciously decide to start a relationship.

You decide to meet someone's needs. What you do for the other person is more important than what they do for you. Genuine love is about meeting another person's needs. Whatever makes them happy, brings peace and ease in life, is a need you can meet. This means actively seeking opportunities to bring happiness into their life, help, and meet needs rather than seeking someone to be your blesser. Love drives you to give while lust and poverty drive you to take, ask, and require things being given to you.

People have increasingly become more self-centred. Only desiring such things that are calculated to make one better and increase their profit from interactions. "What is in it for me?". The key to finding lasting love is to detach from this mindset and ask yourself, "What value will I bring to this person?" "What needs will I meet?". These questions will help you become a high-quality lover and not focus on receiving and being a needy partner.

Love is a lifetime decision. The two of you must intend to spend the rest of your lives together in a loving relationship. If you desire marriage, from the onset of the relationship, this should be your obvious intention, but if you remove this, your relationship becomes a casual one, lacking commitment. I have seen relationships that started as a one-night stand, open relationship, or friends with benefits. After some time, the two became committed and exclusive, desiring to progress towards marriage. The faulty start and faulty foundation of such relationships cause them to be riddled with problems, rarely leading to or into marriage. You should be clear from the beginning of the relationship if both of you want the same thing - marriage.

Commonly, people know what they want from you when they approach you, be it to fulfil their sexual desires or to begin a romantic relationship with the future intention of getting married. If you started on the wrong side with a faulty foundation, I strongly advise you to quit rather than trying to drag it to the right side.

Sometimes it is profitable to buy a new iPhone than to attempt fixing an old one. In particular, a man is seldom unclear about what his objectives are. If all he wants is sex and a good time, that's all he will stop at. Should you want marriage from such, you can never give him sex as a strategy to entice or drag them to the altar. However, should you practise celibacy with him, he will either leave you for those who can give the sex he wants from those who put a price tag on it, hidden or upfront. He also could decide to walk with you and discover more meaningful treasure within you that surpasses what your body can offer in a few minutes of sex. He will change his goals along the way as he finds you desirable for marriage.

Finally, "expecting nothing in return" offers advice on how to manage your expectations in a relationship. Love is not transactional. You cannot expect a gift because you gave a gift. Love does not work like that. I do not expect my wife to do my laundry or cook for me, but each time she does it, I am forever grateful and appreciative. I expect to do things for her. Because she does not owe me any favours, I take nothing she does for me for granted. You can control your own expectations of what you invest in the relationship, not your expectations of your partner. Consistently unmet expectations lead to dissatisfaction and divorce. If you have no expectations of the other, anything that comes your way is a blessing worth celebrating. Stress and frustration are the offspring of unmet expectations in relationships.

If both of you want marriage, be clear from the beginning. Unfortunately, feelings aren't enough for love to work. Love isn't enough for marriage to succeed. Love alone cannot succour the relationship through life experiences, whether good or challenging times.

A marriage begins with love, but it takes more than that to have a delightful marriage and to last until death do you part. Many marriage hopefuls and first timers think or assume that love is the key to marital bliss. I always teach couples that love is not the only key. Love is just one key or foundation on which every happily married couple stands.

John Lennon, in 1967, released a song titled "All You Need Is Love" and in 1968 he divorced. I think he understood the power and importance of love but was deceived into believing that all he needed was love. Love is not all you need. Love is part of what you need to make your relationship and marriage work.

In this book, I will only discuss the reasons love isn't enough. One of my upcoming books will exhaustively discuss other keys to a successful marriage apart from love, which will include wisdom, understanding, and knowledge.

Seven reasons why love is not enough:

1. All divorced couples got married because they loved each other except for arranged marriages and marriages of convenience. If you talk to or observe comments from divorcees, mostly you will hear things like our love had grown cold, disappeared, grew apart, or love had turned bitter. This is not enough to keep them in marriage.

Several weeks ago, I read in a divorce announcement by a celebrity couple that they still loved each other but chose separate paths. How sad that you still have love for the person and can't continue doing marriage together.

2.   The love that starts a relationship is not good enough to grow the relationship into a marriage. The love that begins a marriage will not suffice to keep the marriage happy and free from problems. Love is like a manual vehicle's gear number one; it starts off the vehicle into motion. The vehicle moves forward even on an incline with gear number one only, but you cannot drive from home to work on gear number one. You need all other gears to get to your destination. Without other gears, a ten-mile trip can be an excruciating driving experience with only gear number one. So can be your driving experience if your relationship vehicle only has love.

3.   Love needs nurturing to maturity and only wisdom, knowledge, and understanding for relationships and marriage can grow love to

maturity. Love needs protection from many things, like foolishness in behaviour and words, a harsh environment, and situations. Many are the forces against love than those for you in a love relationship. Love is like a rose plant; it needs tender care to mature and protection to reduce risks of plant disease or physical harm. In maturity, it will develop its own sharp prickles for physical protection, though not enough to deter beetles and mites. Other keys, like wisdom and communication, will protect your love and reduce the risk of falling out of love.

4.   Many people don't understand what love looks like for married people. I have met some innocent people who think it's the butterflies in the tummy while others feel a spark and call it love. Butterflies and sparks lack longevity, hence not good enough for marriage. Love in marriage and love before marriage are worlds apart. You will need to build understanding once you get into marriage on how love for spouses is demonstrated.

5.	Poor communication is good enough to turn love into hurt and anger. Communication problems will make you think your partner loves you less than before. This alone will push you to build assumptions while storing unresolved issues, only to wake up quitting the relationship. Love needs exceptional communication skills to last long enough. If you cannot communicate, you will have unnecessary arguments, and arguing couples are not happy couples. If your partner is a terrible listener, chances of relating well are slim. Good communication offers your relationship a good chance in marriage.

6.	Love does not solve relationship problems. More often, wisdom solves problems and money can settle your relationship problems. My wife and I are opposites almost in everything. Driving together in our old Nissan Livina 2014 model used to be a hustle when temperatures were high. Most of the time she felt cold at my preferred temperature while I felt too much heat at her temperature preference. Instead of fighting about high and low temperatures, we had two options:

either to drive separately and spend more on fuel or to upgrade and buy a vehicle that allows different temperature zones for either side. We took the second option and money solved the problem, though it was wisdom that informed the solution.

7. Love usually suffers in the absence of trust and honesty. People often find themselves in relationships where they love their spouse deeply but cannot trust them. Such relationships are at a high risk of separation because of insecurities, lies, and assumptions. No one enjoys being suspected of wrongdoing by their spouse. When your phone rings, when you come home later than usual, when you miss a call, when going for a business trip or work, social event, all these are trigger signs of mistrust. If you can't trust them before marriage, the ring will not restore the trust. Love easily expires in a marriage that is trust starved.

Chapter 2

Preparing for a wedding over a marriage.

Nowadays, most marriage hopefuls dream of the wedding day, but few dream so vividly about their marriage life. Their vision ends with a planned wedding day, and that is why marriage life and staying in marriage becomes a nightmare experience. Failure to prepare and plan for your marital life is planning your divorce unconsciously. Marital success is not a product of luck or prayer, but intentional planning. Life on earth has a way of effortlessly delivering the bad and ugly pieces of the pie your way, but good things like an argument free marriage are a product of intentional planning and carefully invested effort.

Ask any average couple intending to marry this question; how are you preparing for marriage? Chances are they will overwhelm you with wedding planning details and logistics of moving in together. The venue secured, number of guests, the who's who on the guest list, colour theme, bridal dances, wedding gown, hairstyle, manicure, and the food, yet none of these are marriage related. Wedding plans are not marriage plans. These two are different and cannot be mistaken for the other. Marriage life starts after the wedding. It is more desirable to prepare for life (marriage) than to prepare for a day (wedding). It is called "wedding day" because it's just a single day out of 365 days in a single year out of your decades of life together.

A wedding is not a marriage. A wedding is for the public, yet marriage is only for two people. At a wedding, you both serve other people, but in marriage, you serve each other. A wedding has spectators, while marriage is in private with no spectators. Marriage is a picture of your reality, while weddings are glitzy affairs. You hire people to cook and clean at a wedding, but in marriage, you will both do the cooking and cleaning. A wedding is to celebrate the beginning of a marriage. It has a start and finishing time while marriage has no expiry date.

Weddings end in joy and celebrations with cameras everywhere while the end of a marriage is in sorrow and grief at a gravesite of the spouse or worse off with a divorce, shying away from cameras after the last court session. The wise prioritise long-term rewards over short-term enjoyment. Only shallow lovers plan and invest in weddings over their marriage.

Because of the maverick views of today's young adults, the divorce rate is at an all-time high. Couples plan a wedding but inadequately plan and prepare for marriage. Weddings keep getting more and more sophisticated, stylish, and expensive, while marriages continue to sustain increased blows, unending fiascos, and divorce rates. It is an error, ignorance, blunder, and a costly mistake to spend thousands of dollars on a wedding for three hours and spend nothing preparing for a lifetime in marriage. Premarital counselling is the best way to prepare for your marriage. Engaging the services of a great counsellor will cost you, but it is worth all the financial and time investment.

Have you ever entered an exam room unprepared? Imagine a scenario where the invigilator passes by you, checks your answer sheet, and announces to everyone. "Make sure you read the question carefully before answering!" Your lack of preparation will land you in a deep panic tank, err, and guarantee poor marks. For the prepared student, this is a welcome caution and shows the invigilator wishes you well. If you enter marriage unprepared, even the things that should grow your intimacy can be your stumbling blocks.

Your understanding of marriage life informs your choice of whom to wed. In 2021, I facilitated a memorable workshop series for single ladies themed single ladies dilemma. A greater portion of the attendants had a checklist of their right guy for marriage. Going through the list, I would ask questions like, what benefit would this item contribute to your marriage life? It did not surprise me that there was no explanation for most of the listed items. This exercise, however, exposed how shallow many singles intending to marry sadly prepare for marriage. It is a reality that most single ladies are more conscious and intentional about their wedding event than the life after.

A tall, dark, and handsome guy is in high demand, but what value to you and your marriage is the height and complexion? If you are marrying for superb wedding pics and Instagram couple goals, then all these are salient for you. However, if you desire a happy and fulfilling marriage, you need to prioritise other critical aspects. Character, religion, beliefs, values, mentality, ambitions, and purpose are all critical for marriage yet are not picture friendly for wedding and Instagram pictures.

It is a perplexing reality that some women begin their wedding plans before they've found the groom - are they so keen to get down the aisle only or the marriage life too? She knows the dress she will wear, the venue, the cake she wants, whom not to invite, and the photo shoot, now all she needs is the husband to be. Nothing wrong with this, but only if more people could plan and prepare for their marriage life in advance like their weddings, we would have the same success rate in marriage as we do at weddings.

Bishop David Oyedepo once said you are not ready for marriage until you have read seven good books on marriage. This is very true. Instead of having a seven-tier cake or seven bridesmaids in a seven-star hotel and riding in a seven series at your wedding, invest in seven books that will help you enjoy your marriage. Instead of hosting a debt-funded wedding, rather enrol for a premarital counselling course and or buy books and study your way to a blissful marriage.

You can agree, this isn't the popular or preferred way to spend your financial resources, since your family, colleagues, and friends are expecting a spectacular wedding. You may also have some subtle pressure to host a better wedding than the last wedding you attended of a relative or friend. Don't be one of those people who overdo it for the wedding because you feel some competition and want to impress guests.

Do not consider people's opinions of your wedding. This will cause financial problems for you even before the marriage starts. I know a couple who could not leave the wedding venue as service providers, including the venue manager, blocked them demanding payments. The newly-weds had promised to settle the balance before the end of the wedding party. The couple hoped to collect cash gifts from their guest, which fell short of expectations. Some conversations you should never have in the first few days of your marriage, and debt or financial pressure is one of them.

Many couples hardly enjoy their weddings, but guests do. Instead of a wedding for guests to enjoy, you will be wise to invest in your marriage by acquiring knowledge. I am not against weddings or their beauty; they are necessary. I think a wedding is not worth the effort if it will be at the expense of investing in your marriage. In the church I serve in, by wisdom, the Senior Pastor has simplified weddings in such a way that couples have great weddings for less than $500 USD while they spend time and money preparing for marital bliss.

Your wedding is the first project you and your spouse will manage together and it's an accurate reflection of the lifestyle and choices you will make in the future for your family. If your wedding leaves you in debt, chances are you will live a life of debt from your choices. If you choose a venue or gown or vehicles to transport you based on the perception you want your guests to have of you, chances are in your marriage you will continue with the same pattern and stay in a suburb or drive a car to satisfy what people will say or think about you.

Let your wedding show your wisdom. If you have no life savings to start your family on, then you have no business doing an expensive wedding. Be wise and live your size per time. They deceived you into thinking that other people's opinions about your wedding matter; they don't. Your relatives and friends have a right to own their opinion, and it does not add or subtract anything from your marriage. If the same person was to suggest to you not to wed your fiancé, you would strongly disagree, feel offended, argue it's not their decision to make, and you would ignore their opinion. How then is it their views of your wedding day now matter to you? Instead of spending a lot on a wedding or gown you will wear only for 3 hours, rather spend more on marriage preparation and a longer honeymoon doing fun activities together.

When you are married, you will become one, his and hers, yours and mine mentality will need to shift to us and them. This is a mystery taught in God's word and is the best way for your marriage to have a chance of success. One avenue you will become one is by managing your assets and finances together for the family. Do not get married if you are not happy with the concept of managing your income contributions to the family together. Planning your wedding together may be a good indicator of your mindset and that of your partner towards managing finances.

A wedding is beautiful, but a costly wedding is not a worthwhile endeavour if your combined financial situation has considerable liabilities, college debt, cars, credit cards, etc… Wisdom should advise you to work on getting out of debt and improving your new family's financial situation.

The cost of your wedding does not reflect the quality of your relationship nor determine marital happiness. Some couples spend all their money on a wedding only to move into an empty apartment. A certain young couple had to borrow a bed on the way back from their honeymoon after a nice wedding. A sad reflection of the couple's wisdom at work. Ask yourself this question: What is the main purpose of my wedding? The purpose of a wedding is simply to join you and your fiancée together (marriage) before God and witnesses. How much will that cost you? That will be your justifiable wedding cost and anything above this will be your wants, not your needs, for the wedding day. Do not go broke to finance your luxuries.

Don't let your wedding day fool you into thinking it's the most important day of your life. It is not. There are many other days more important than your wedding day, such as the day you were born, the day you were born again and received the life of Christ, and the day you discover your purpose (the reason you are alive).

Signs that you value wedding preparations over marital preparations:

1. **Time** - when you have time to research for a wedding venue and wedding service providers but no time to research counselling services, time for wedding rehearsals and bridal dances, but no time to attend premarital counselling sessions.

2. **Money** - when paying for counselling services is not a priority over securing a skilled photographer for your wedding or the best caterer in town.

3. **Effort** - having a detailed plan for the wedding, while learning about marriage at random.

4. **Words** - when your close family and friends only know about your wedding plans and nothing

about your marital preparation through premarital counselling.

5. **Resolve or determination** - when you solve every challenge thrown at your wedding plans, yet any minor challenge to your marital preparations is enough for you to give up.

Chapter 3

Premarital cohabitation is a step closer to marriage.

The term cohabitation refers to an arrangement in which two people who are not married live and are sexually involved together. Depending on the relationship design, it could be permanent, long-term, short-term, and with or without the intention of marriage. Those who cohabit as their final destination understand exactly what they want and easily obtain such. Those who cohabit with an intention to marry short-change themselves. It is a fallacy to cohabit, hoping to strengthen the relationship into marriage.

Cohabitation has risen dramatically and quickly in many European countries, the USA, South Africa, Zimbabwe, and across the globe. As cohabitation has increased, so has the amount of sociological research devoted to it. The only problem is that no one is talking about the research findings on premarital cohabitation. Most people are deaf to these findings, or the traditional media industry is biased in what it broadcasts. Several credible research findings have reported more cons than pros to cohabitation.

Author's Galena K. Rhoades, Scott M. Stanley, and Howard J. Markman published their research findings titled "Couples' Reasons for Cohabitation: Associations with Individual Well-Being and Relationship Quality". They cited these three main reasons people go into cohabitation: time together, convenience, and testing. Let's explore these three reasons. From their findings, cohabiting partners often had a motive to test whether the marriage will work with their partner. I think this is a wrong test for anyone to employ in predicting marital success. Marriage is only successful when all the conditions to make marriage work are present, and cohabitation lacks the fundamental conditions, including the most basic one: a lifetime commitment.

Cohabitation is not like a mock exam, where the marks count or do not count, which serves primarily as practice for future exams. It's your life we're talking about, and you only have one life to live. There's no time to experiment or practise with the limited days you have at your disposal. If the primary goal for cohabitation is to test, how do you allow someone to test drive on you before buying?

The only products anyone may test on are called samples and they are not what the customer goes home with. If you allow yourself to be tested on, low are the chances of them taking you to the altar.

Choose to not be a test drive option for someone. You are unique and custom made for someone serious to take you without a test drive. People only test something they are uncertain of. If they are not sure, then they should be respectful enough to leave you for someone who will be sure and not require testing.

In 2020, I bought a C200 Mercedes Benz, but I tested three other vehicles. Even though I knew what I wanted, I still enjoyed testing others, fully aware I was not taking them home. The same is with some people when they cohabit with you hiding behind testing, yet they already know they will not marry you but still want to enjoy you. This explains why some people cohabit for two years or more with no sight of the wedding day.

The same is when you go for wine tasting, you can get drunk and enjoy the joy of testing different varieties with no commitment. Should you wish to order a bottle of wine in a restaurant, they can give you a tester, and it is usually a single sip, but cohabitation is not a sip, it is giving the full bottle to test with a hope they will like it and choose to pay.

If this were the case with restaurants, they would have made losses and shut down. Cohabitation will shut down your marriage dream.

After several failed cohabitations, many lose hope of marriage. This is because cohabitation is not testing anything about marriage but simply offering yourself as though in "marriage" without the full benefits of a marital relationship that you so deserve. Cohabitation is like being employed in a supermarket and performing the responsibilities of a store manager while on a store assistant salary, hoping the owner will like you and compensate you fairly. It's a losing arrangement. If the owner can get all your services for less, why would they pay more? Even if you were the owner, I bet you wouldn't change a thing from this arrangement.

How many people do you want to test before deciding? How long should the test be? What items exactly are being tested? Is there a monthly review of how the test subject is performing? How do you know if the test subject has passed or failed? Who moderates the test? Is it possible to test two candidates at once? In case they fail the test, do they get another chance to test and correct their errors? All these and others are all questions that will never have satisfactory answers regarding cohabitation. You are better single than onboard a sinking ship. Cohabitation is a sinking ship. Like the Titanic, a few may survive but their lives were never the same after the traumatic experience, so is with a break up from a cohabitation relationship.

The second popular reason from the research findings was that people cohabit to spend more time together. I think people should maximise their singleness while it lasts as marriage will be a lifetime journey. How much time do you need to spend with this person for you to know them? I am sure it's not overnight while you are sleeping.

If this person cannot create time to see you, take you on dates, book out their Saturday for you, then surely, they will not do it when you are married. You would only get to see each other at night if you worked the same daytime hours. That sounds like they value time spent with you before going to bed and when you wake up. They are more interested in bedtime.

Convenience is the last reason people cohabit, according to the research's finding. Unfortunately, we have become a generation of people who want quick and easy things in life unlike the preceding generations. No wonder why we are having more failed relationships and marriages than in the past.

Some things just don't change. Marriage still requires sacrifices to function; romantic relationships thrive on sacrifice as a show of love. The direct opposite of sacrifice is convenience. If convenient, your relationship will last. If not convenient, then you find another partner in-convenience. Any relationship based on convenience cannot weather any storm and only last until the convenience expires. Every married person will confess that inconveniences are common and the more you embrace them, the more you will enjoy.

Majority of conveniences are financial, such as sharing accommodation, a car, bills, and responsibilities. You deserve a relationship with someone who chooses you all the time, in good and in challenging times. I have heard heart-breaking stories of breakups because the conveniences have become a burden like a partner losing their income stream, sickness, and many others. You can save yourself the trouble by taking the wisdom shared in this book. Do not let your bank account decide and push you into cohabitation, rather soldier on now and have a model marriage in the future.

Waiting for the right time can be inconvenient. It is called patience. Patience is a virtue and good things still come to those who wait. Jean-Jacques Rousseau said,

"Patience is bitter, but its fruit is sweet". Every romantic relationship feeds on the patience of the two individuals. You need someone patient with you in your weaknesses and you also need to exercise patience towards them. If he or she is not patient enough to wait for marriage, he or she may not be patient enough to work on the relationship in the future to overcome any challenges.

Do not assume the difference between cohabitation and marriage is a signed piece of paper. No! You are full of ignorance if you think so. Recognizing as married is too deep and has benefits that cohabitation can never compare to. Married couples are more faithful, act in the best interest of their spouse, tell the truth more than cohabiting partners, handle money responsibly and think long term compared to cohabiting partners.

I think if you weaken these five things from a romantic relationship, you would have robbed yourself of what you deserve. You are worth it, more than what cohabitation offers. Do not settle for anything less than your desired marriage. It is not good enough to say that it is a step in the right direction or that half a loaf is better than none when you have the potential to get a whole loaf. In marriage, half a loaf will frustrate you to the divorce court.

The difference between living with a spouse and a cohabiting partner is like buying pants from Fabiani and buying pants from a low-quality Chinese shop. They may look the same. People may not immediately see the difference but give it your first wash and you will see the low-quality pants losing colour while Fabiani still looks great. In cohabiting, you have little chance of weathering any wash simply because there is no commitment to stick it out, which is like a quality guarantee you get from Fabiani. Most low-quality products stores have no returns, no refunds, and no exchange policy for a reason.

During my college days, I once bought sweatpants in a low-quality products China store in the Cape Town CBD for sports day games. I ripped the sweatpants upon stretching on the same day. Upon returning to the shop, they simply showed me a handwritten notice that said No returns, No exchanges, No guarantees, and No refunds. It's not that I didn't see the sign before purchasing, but I simply ignored it. Maybe I thought I was special, and that I could get away with the low-quality sweatpants. The same is with people who cohabit, they assume they are special, and their relationship is different, so they will manage and have a happy ending, ignoring all the clear written signs of trouble ahead.

The sweatpants failed to last a day in use, over 50% of cohabitation relationships do not last a year. Had the sweatpants lasted their first use, I do not think they would be good to wear after their first wash. Cohabiting relationships do not have a sound foundation that can last a relationship storm. When my sweatpants tore, shame and embarrassment gripped me. Luckily, the games were being played near my place of residence on campus, and I hastily went to my room and changed.

I learned a lesson not to repeat on that day. A cheap price on a low-quality product is a sign of danger. In a cohabiting relationship, you are simply a storm away from your heartbreak. Your relationship does not have the fabric for relationship challenges. So easily, people break off their cohabiting arrangements. The heartbreak, hurt, sense of failure, disappointment, anger, etc… are all feelings that are certain for a failed cohabiting relationship. The effort is not worth the trauma.

How dump and still be breathing could I be? Had I gone to buy another pair from the same shop? In relationships, I have observed that very few people learn from mistakes. Many folks today still repeat the same mistake, ill-informed strategy, and expect a different result. How many people can you cohabit with before you quit and do the right thing? Can you imagine if a girl or boy you want to date confided in you about having lived with three other people before you and that each of those relationships had lasted between three and eighteen months? You would not feel good or hopeful after this brief cohabiting history. If it was you having cohabited three times with different partners, I am sure you would erase some names from this history file or mark it as a classified file of your past that no one should access.

Prior research on cohabitation identified it as a risk factor for divorce in marriage. Despite now being an acceptable cultural norm, premarital cohabitation is still a risk factor for divorce today. In a study published in 2019 in the Journal of Marriage and Family, Michael Rosenfeld, and Katharina Roesler's findings show there is an increased risk of divorce for those who cohabit pre-marriage than those who do not. According to their conclusion, premarital cohabitation may have short-term benefits but long-term costs for marital stability and is not an appropriate marriage path to experiment with.

In their decades-long research, they also found out that premarital cohabitation has low divorce odds in the first year, but from year two and forever, the divorce rate is higher than couples who never cohabited before marriage. This clearly shows that premarital cohabitation is a seed planted and its bitter fruit harvest will be in marriage. From several other studies done, it is crystal clear that premarital cohabitation is not a viable step closer to marriage, but a setup for a failed future marriage.

There are many reasons premarital cohabitation is a step backward not forward, one being that once you move in together, it becomes too hard to break it off as too much intertwining would have happened, and people eventually flow with the idea of marriage ignoring all red flag signs. Red flags unresolved become intolerable problems tomorrow. Axinn and Barber (1997) showed that premarital cohabitation weakens a person's attitudes about marriage and divorce, lowers esteem for marriage, and increases tolerance and acceptance of divorce.

White (1990), postulates that people who have been previously married, married young, whose parents are divorced, who have lived together prior to marriage or had children before marriage are less likely to maintain their marriages. According to White, of all the five influences listed above, I see that you have direct control over four factors. Only the divorce of your parents had no input from you hence you had no control over that. Your direct input the other four factors including cohabitation can be changed should you seek to improve your odds in marriage.

Lastly, the main reason premarital cohabitation has a higher probability of marital failure is that the marriage started on a weaker foundation. As a girlfriend, boyfriend, or partner, you have less accountability, commitment, sacrifices, and you are less compelled to fight for the relationship compared to married folk. Signing the marriage certificate does not automatically upgrade these to high marital standards, and cohabiting many couples cannot negotiate this transition. After your honeymoon, you will realise your husband or wife on paper is still behaving and talking like the boyfriend or girlfriend you cohabited with before the wedding, yet you now require spousal treatment.

You can't teach an old horse a new trick and in relationships, this is also true. I think it is easier to sell ice to an Eskimo than to request changes from your spouse over something that you have been ok with for the past year or two cohabiting. They typically perceive this as you are trying to control and change them or that you have changed instead of your spouse realising the relationship situation has changed. Couples that try to change each other do not stay together.

How to avoid premarital cohabitation:

1. **Become financially independent.** When people face difficulties, such as dealing with their own bills, extended family needs, etc… cohabitation becomes a viable financial option. If you can take care of your needs, then nothing will compel you to cohabit. If you cohabit because of financial reasons, you will struggle to leave the partner even when you know the relationship is not working. Your logic will convince you to stay, a soft life voice will remind you that all the luxuries and the new lifestyle conveniences will cease.

    I met a lady who was in a cohabitation situation; she advised she can't leave the man because since she moved in with him, she can now take care of her ailing mother as he takes care of most of their bills. Cohabitation should not be your income generating or saving business plan, become financially independent and maintain a sober life of unbiased choices as you journey to marriage.

    Instead of staying with a partner, rather stay with a friend or relative and share costs with no strings attached. It is better to stay in your parent's house than to cohabit.

2. **Premarital celibacy.** Determine to reserve sex for marriage. There is no cohabitation without sexual relations. I have dedicated the next chapter to discuss the sex topic and I pray you see the method to my madness.

3. **Delayed gratification.** Good things come to those who wait. Everything is good and beautiful in its due season. A powerful lesson we get from nature is that every fruit tastes bitter until it is ripe. Your relationship is only ripe in marriage. That is where its fruit becomes a delicacy.

   Animals do not eat unripe fruit by choice, they wait until the fruit is palatable. Think of a monkey and how much it enjoys the banana fruit, yet it waits patiently until it is ripe. Learn the habit of delaying gratification.

4. **Marry young.** If you are old enough to cohabit you are old enough to marry, anything else is an excuse no matter how much you add sense to it.

Never despise humble beginnings. Do not delay marriage on account of material possessions. If you have an income source and meet your own bills in a month without your parent's help, then you qualify to marry. Anything above this is a luxury in your head and not a necessity.

In most countries, the minimum legal age to marry is eighteen years. This is how I interpret this; from eighteen years, the government trusts you enough to make conscious permanent decisions. A decision that can produce another human life into this world. If you are over eighteen years, then your age is not reason enough to delay marriage. If you think the age of your spouse matters, then I think this minimum legal age should also matter to you.

Marrying young is beautiful, but only for those who have financial independence from their parents. You cannot try to marry young to increase your parent's monthly expenses. Such a thing shows your lack of responsibility, immaturity, and poor decision-making patterns (foolishness). In post Covid years, there are many dynamics for marriage and family income so I would say at least one of you should make enough income to sustain your monthly expenses as a couple. If I had written this book decades ago, I would have strictly said the husband should earn enough for the family, but nowadays family dynamics accommodate stay home dads.

Marrying young and staying with your partner does not drastically increase your living expenses while kids come with increased expenditure. You can marry young and delay kids until you have increased your financial comfort to whatever level you desire. When I married, I was staying in a one-bedroom apartment and my wife moved in after the wedding. We stayed there for nearly two years before moving to a much bigger place. We had no car when we married, and we used to take a bus together for commuting and now we can afford one. You can still achieve your goals after the wedding and marriage. Do not delay marriage.

As partners, you display a special level of loyalty and sacrifice in the days of humble beginnings. The days when you are still figuring out things are unique, but in your days of abundance, friends are many. If they loved and married you with no wealth, you can be sure that you will build wealth together. I think couples that worked hard together have more beautiful and rich memories of loyalty than those who started out in abundance. If you can find joy with little or no options, you have a better chance to enjoy with more options. However, most who start with abundance and many options in life often wonder if their relationship can survive lack.

As much as marrying young is a beautiful thing, I give a strong caution to those who wish to consider this. Young is usually associated with lack of wisdom while we assume the old to be wise. There is wisdom that comes by age, and it's not to be despised. If you choose to marry young, your wisdom should be mature for marriage. Your wisdom should strongly come from books, marriage counsellors, and mentors who are successful in marriage. Once you have gained enough wisdom to make marriage work, you can be sure to be successful in marriage than older folks who have no wisdom but scars from many past failed relationships.

I have a lovely sister, five years older than I. A while back, while preparing food in the kitchen, we happened to have a random conversation with our granny. Granny inquired of my sister's age and, to her surprise, my sister was twenty years old and still single. Granny got married at sixteen and thought my sister was delaying marriage unnecessarily. She offered to help my sister marry, as this marriage delay case in her mind was dire. See, from the twentieth century going backwards, people used to marry young and never divorce.

Today we delay marriage all the way to forty years. Midlife crisis kicks in while others are still newly-weds. Nonetheless, many of today's couples divorce even before their wedlock child graduates from kindergarten. That's a quick in and out in marriage terms.

My granny married at sixteen and remained married for almost seventy years before grandpa went to be with the Lord. They owed their marital success to the knowledge they received from their auntie's, uncles, parents, and old-fashioned marital classes before the marriage. She gained marital knowledge at sixteen that was ample for her marriage. Today, I am not surprised to hear a thirty-two-year-old asking questions like, why should I submit to my husband? Others argue that their phone is their privacy, their wife should not touch it. No wonder marriage is fast becoming a muddle.

I encourage you to marry young and full of wisdom to make your marriage work. There are countless benefits to marrying young, like having a good chance to marry a virgin or as a virgin yourself. Marrying young confer better chances of finding someone with no or less baggage from unhealed wounds in past relationships. Growing and learning together in life is beautiful than marrying someone who has missed the better part of your adult life.

The bible in Proverbs 5:18-19 Amplified Bible says, "Let your fountain (wife) be blessed [with the rewards of fidelity] And rejoice in the wife of your youth. Let her be as a loving hind and graceful doe, let her breasts refresh and satisfy you at all times; Always be exhilarated and delight in her love."

The wife of your youth means you are married while in your youthful days. The United Nations define youth as those persons between the age of fifteen and twenty-four years old. Many are missing the opportunity to enjoy their youth with their husband or wife. Many gave their youth to people who never valued them, that's why they never married them. Marrying young ensures you give your youth to the only person who is willing to do life with you to old age.

Do not marry old. Young is great for a robust sex life. In the bible verse above, we describe a youthful wife as a doe, a female deer. A doe is synonymous with agility and speed, can reach about eighty kilometres per hour and jump in excess of two metres in height. Marrying in your youth ensures you do not miss out on bedroom fireworks as your spouse unleashes the deer in them. Do not cut corners for an experience with stolen waters, marry your own, and rejoice in the marriage bed with the spouse of your youth. Later in life, many will be the cares of life, children, reduced libido, and other health issues, like erectile dysfunction.

Kelani Karamat, published with the International Journal of Social Science and Humanity in 2016; Perceptions on Implications of Delayed Marriage: A Case Study of Married Adults in Kuala Lumpur. The study discovered that people who postpone marriage have a proclivity to begin engaging in premarital sexual behaviour. For this reason, the risk of acquiring sexually transmitted diseases and infections, including HIV is very high among never-married people compared to currently married people. (Karamat, 2016). Do not delay marriage.

Marry as soon as possible. Only start a relationship when you are ready to marry and quickly decide to marry. I think this is very important to avoid falling into the cohabitation trap. If you know you are not planning to marry in the next two years, then stay out of relationships. When you drag your courtship phase, you will start seeing no reason to not stay together, yet you still see reasons not to marry.

Your partner is not a college degree that takes three- or four-year's study time. You will not know everything about your partner because you haven't married them. Courtship should only give you a glimpse of what lies ahead. I think six months is a good enough time for you to decide if this is the right person for you or not. A year to two years is the maximum reasonable courtship period before the wedding. Anything above this is an unnecessary delay.

A sure way to not enter a relationship that has goals that are SMART-less is to be frank with your partner at the beginning. Ask them questions like, when do you intend to marry? The goal must be time bound. If your marriage clock is saying you are now due or long overdue for marriage, you have little time to waste. This means you should be upfront with the conversation and explain how long you can be patient and make an effort to marry sooner before your patience is tested.

I recently watched a Netflix reality show called "The Ultimatum", the partners on the show had been together for close to two or more years and yet the other partner was not ready to marry and had to be given an ultimatum to force a decision. Only one relationship had no cohabitation. The longer you delay marriage, the more accepting you may become of cohabiting.

Delaying marrying means you are not ready to commit to this person you are with. It also means you may not be sure that you have the right person. It can also mean you have not dealt with past relationship failures and fear disappointment. I strongly advise couples to discuss their goals and any reasoning behind certain decisions.

Chapter 4

You need sex experience before marriage.

We are living in an era where the sex-positive movement is flourishing, and the subject is no longer taboo, unlike in the past. We have seen an increase in acceptance of and tolerance for premarital sex because of the invention of condoms as a "safe sex" option against HIV, STIs, and pregnancies.

If you can have sex and not get an STI, HIV, or pregnancy, then what are you waiting for? Why wait for marriage? After all, are you not free to do as you wish with your body? These questions have become popular, and we have termed sex "safe" if you use a condom, but forgetting that sex before marriage is not safe for marriage. Be of a sober mind, having sex before marriage is not a norm. You can be one of the many who plan to save it for marriage.

There are only two ways to deceive a person: either make them believe a lie or make them deny the truth. One of the dangerous deceptions being peddled by social media and the mainstream media is the acceptance and normalisation of sex before marriage. Many singles in our generation think that it is ok to have consensual sex with anyone whom you choose to and whenever you wish. Indeed, we are free-willed beings, but all our choices have consequences.

Sex experience is the only experience in life that has no glory, and your spouse will not celebrate you for having a long list of sexual partners and diverse sexual encounters, they rather fall into suspicion that you have zipping up issues which raises insecurities in the relationship.

A certain proverb says, "you have to kiss a lot of frogs before you meet your handsome prince". I don't think you have to kiss any frog; you can aim to kiss your prince at the altar. If you see that it is a frog, do not kiss it, even if it wears a tuxedo. If sex was a vacancy (position) in marriage, the job specification would say "strictly no experience required or zero experience would be advantageous". The less experience you have, the better it is for you and for your spouse in marriage.

A certain marriage ended in divorce simply because the husband had many premarital sexual experiences with kinky ladies in past relationships. Some introduced him to anal sex. He soon learned that his wife wasn't as wild as the other girls after a few months in marriage. His developed passion for anal sex became increasingly difficult for him to ignore, but his wife was strongly against anal sex. His vaginal sexual satisfaction dwindled and felt anal would complete the circuit while his wife was bordering between disappointment and shock from her husband's expectations of her in bed. She always told him she was not like his other past girls and suggested not to compare her. Their sex life issues became louder and weakened the marriage to divorce.

Had he maintained zero sex experience until marriage, all he would know was his wife and she would be his best for life. As a lady, if you test other penis sizes and skills of other sex exper-vets (expert + pervert) you will have a high chance of comparing your spouse to your previous sex experiences or expect them to perform things they do not know how to. The penis differs in size (girth, length, and shape). You are safe to learn and enjoy the size you married compared to having prior encounters. You already come in with expectations mostly premised on how you enjoyed or the lack of enjoyment in the past. A spouse who has had many sexual partners is hard to please sexually.

In premarital counselling, I sometimes observe the other person feeling insecure because of their partner's elaborate sexual experience, while they have none. Often, the virgin partner, especially the husband to be, always wonders if he will perform sex to their wife better than the previous partner or partners.

What a joy it will be for you and your spouse after saving sex for marriage and exploring it together? I know of women who fake orgasms to appear like they are enjoying sex, yet they are not enjoying as much as they did with other sexual partners and can't tell their husband to do it like Todd used to slap and choke her. Sexual experience is unpleasant for your future marriage from any angle you may look at it.

I read an article by a marriage and family therapist where the Doctor. said, "Having sexual fantasies of someone other than your spouse is completely natural and normal,". This is the epitome of deception. Such is not natural and is a serious deception with ripple effects leading to divorce. How on earth or on the bed can you be thinking of someone else you had sex with in the past, as if it's the same person you are currently having sex with and it's normal? Answer this question: what would you do or say should your spouse tell you they were thinking of their ex during sex?

As a man or woman thinks so they are, fantasies are desires, thoughts, and imaginations before they become a reality. Surely, they will come to pass, but when it happens, we will know it as cheating. Cheating does not start in bed with another person, but in your mind and heart, the act is simply a manifestation of what's in a person's heart.

I have heard stories of couples having sex and in the climax of the encounter, the other spouse mentions the name of another person they were fantasising about. Usually the fantasy is about a sexual partner from the past. Only a few relationships can survive such a conundrum. All because you had sexual encounters before your spouse and those encounters are still in your head, how do you think your partner will feel or understand this? Would you agree that cheating your spouse in this way is a marital crime that is hard to police?

Sex is different for everyone. People are not machines that are one size fits all. Each person is unique, and your previous experiences easily become a hurdle to learning how your partner appreciates and performs sex uniquely. Please do not fall prey to the illusion that your experiences will benefit your marriage more than they will hurt it.

The media today is pushing an agenda to normalise premarital sex. Seldom can you watch a Hollywood movie or series that has no sex or nudity scenes? Until recently, most productions not only had sex scenes outside marriage but have since upgraded their inclusion levels from heterosexual scenes to homosexual scenes. Better if it were sex between a married couple, but almost all the sex scenes are between strangers, people who met that night, co-workers, and any other sort of unmarried relationship.

For the married, sex is boring, while for singles it's pictured as fun. This is the same as telling unmarried people to have more passionate sex while telling married couples to retire from sex and focus on parenting and housework. This is a deception; it may give you your desires in the present but will take away your glee when it matters the most.

A sexual act expresses a deep intimacy that already exists, not the means of creating a non-existent intimacy. You do not have sex with someone to build intimacy. If intimacy was not there before the sexual act, surely after the act all you will have been two tired people who released body fluid and not intimate people. We create intimacy, nurture it, and sustain it through verbal, emotional connection with, over a time drawing closer to each other. Commitment, trust, honesty, love, sacrifice, and patience are the hallmarks of genuine intimacy, and these have nothing to do with sex, meaning sex is not a measure of closeness and attachment.

You do not have to engage in sex to be close and attached to someone. Sex is irrelevant to how close or how much you love a person. I have family and friends that are very close and attached to me, love me so much without a shadow of doubt, but there is no sex involved. Most of your quality relationships have nothing to do with sex. Before marriage, you do not have to engage in sex with someone to know them, to be close to them, or build a deeper connection–NO!

Do not deceive yourself into thinking if you love each other, then you must have sex. Sex is a physical act where two genital organs come into contact; this is simple biology. Soon after college, I shared a flat with a guy named Zach (not his real name). Zach was in his early 30s and a very hard-working young man. Monday to Friday, he maintained a life of focus, but come Friday and Saturday night, he was a different animal.

Zach would bring home a different woman each night for Friday and Saturday and relax on a Sunday to resume his work-life again on Monday. Thus, two different-sex partners each week, eight in a month and a shocking ninety six plus sex partners in a year. If you still think sex builds intimacy and is a show of love, then someone deceived you for free. Sex was just like a recreational drug for Zach. Do not be someone's detoxing solution after a busy week.

They will put a ring on it if they love you. If they love you, they will take you to the altar in public, not their bedroom, and lock the door in secrecy. If you think having sex with someone will make them love you, then you need a complete change of mind. Man and woman can have sex with anyone and never care to know their name. Sex is not a sign of relationship growth. If not married, sex at best, is a means to a sexual release, a sign of weak morals, diminished self-control, or just a biological and physical   experience. You sure can wait for this lady or gentleman to vow their love for you before God and man before you can give them the best of you.

Sex for human beings is not like sex for animals. Animals have sex mainly for procreation, but with us, sex is multi-dimensional. Sex is intended for pleasure; God created these two organs with this purpose in mind, hence they automatically match like a bolt and nut with no need for new inventions. This is one of the best gifts you can reserve and give to your husband or wife, not some person who will forget your name as soon as you are out of sight.

My wife and I love Judge Lauren lakes' Paternity Court TV show. I have seen many court sessions where the lady is sure they were in love hence they had sex, but the potential father is clear that it was just a prolonged fling, nowhere near a relationship. Sex before marriage is not a sign of commitment to you, but a lack of commitment.

The perfect order of events is simple. They must commit first on the **Altar** before the **Bed** and **Children**, letter A is before letter B, and C in alphabetical order for a reason. Many have tried to reinvent the alphabetical order and found disappointment. Left in rejection with a permanent letter C, the partner moved on to another letter B alternative and never reached letter A with you. Your youth is too short to experiment with, follow the A, B, and C of love relationships, and you will have no regrets in life.

Sex has nothing to do with love. You do not go to bed to make love. You do not make love in 30 minutes. Love is not a creation of sex. If the sex was not satisfying, then what type of love did you make? We need to rise above such silly deceptions and understand what love is and call sex by its name because that is all it is and all it can ever be - sex. If you have sex to make love, how much sex must you have to make enough love? If your partner needs more love, is it ok for them to have sex with more people to harvest more love? If you do not have sex in a week, have you fallen out of love?

Let the truth in this book liberate you from sexual deceptions. Laumann, Gagnon, Michael, and Michaels, 1994 (Edward O. Laumann et al., The Social Organization of Sexuality: Sexual Practices in the United States, (Chicago: University of Chicago Press, 1994), p. 503-505.) conducted a highly esteemed study on sexual behaviour in America and discovered a strong connection between premarital sex and elevated risk of divorce in marriage.

The authors came up with these several conclusions:

1. The first marriage between a virgin bride and virgin groom was dramatically more stable than non-virgins.

2. Those who married as virgins have lower divorce and separation rates than those who were not virgins.

3. Those who marry as non-virgins are also more likely–all other things being equal–to be unfaithful over the rest of their life compared to those spouses who got married while virgins.

4. Those who are virgins at marriage go to greater lengths to avoid divorce and to honour their marriage vows.

5. There is a higher prevalence of marital infidelity among those who engaged in premarital sex, which is assumed to be an important factor in their higher likelihood of divorce.

6.   Essentially, non-virgins typically appear to do more to harm their marriages, and virgins do more to strengthen their marriages.

Ten benefits of premarital celibacy:

1.   People who delay sex for marriage have self-control or self-mastery. This quality alone is a sign telling you that your partner will control their attitude, words, behaviour, and relationships with the opposite sex, and have control over other areas of their life like finances. All these will make your marriage solid with a strong chance to overcome any challenge while avoiding many.

2.   Premarital celibacy allows you to get to know each other, the real you and them, without your thinking, clouded by the physical. You will have a lifetime to know each other sexually, but start your relationship with true intimacy.

3.   Mostly, women often do not engage in sex without establishing an emotional connection, and once sex occurs, they become more attached to the partner. In this state, many cannot notice

any red flag signs until it is too late. Celibacy will keep you from this form of impaired vision.

4.   It is easier to walk away from a platonic relationship than a relationship subdued by sexual encounters and where the sexual act is central to the relationship. I spoke to a lady who just got dumped and her greatest regret was opening her legs for him all too early. She felt like he robbed her of something, but she never felt like that when she broke up with her first boyfriend, though they were together much longer and were celibate.

5.   Should the relationship fail without sex, I can assure you it wouldn't have lasted in marriage, which is a plus for you. You avoided knowing too late that the relationship wouldn't last. Sex has the effect of delaying an imminent break-up.

6.   You and your partner will not have trust issues, celibacy and faithfulness are sure signs that your spouse will be trustworthy in marriage. Many couples that struggle with trust know their partner could not and did not wait for marriage to have sex. Trust is a big deal in marriage. Many in marriage could sacrifice anything just to have the

assurance they can trust their spouse. If your guy could not wait to touch your breast after the wedding, it will be hard for you to think he will resist any other breast offer from a lady crushing on him.

7.   Studies have shown spouses who remained celibate until marriage found that they were more satisfied sexually than those who indulged in sexual activity before marriage.

8.   You will not be alone on your waiting journey. Most people who wait are likely to marry another who waited or who is prepared to wait with them.

9.   Your relationship progresses faster and matures quicker. Couples who engage in early premarital sex normally find their relationship underdeveloped after a long period, they are slow to learn non-physical ways to express love and eventually take longer to commit to marriage. Waiting helps you perfect your communication skills as a couple and brings stability to your relationship.

10.   A clear conscience is priceless. Knowing you have no sex history and memories you can not disclose to your spouse is a great place to be in

marriage. After celibacy, you will find your first sex encounter significantly satisfying and worth the wait.

I am convinced that celibacy in singles yields delicacy in marriage while sex results in more sex exes. There is an important distinction to make here: waiting until marriage to have sex includes not only virgins on the wedding night but also anyone who has previously had sex in prior relationships or marriages but has remained celibate in their current situation until the wedding night.

I have sat with couples in my office and smell that the other spouse or both suspect each other of cheating and cannot vouch for each other's faithfulness. This used to boggle my mind, as I could not get any reason to justify the doubt or the allegations level against the other spouse. All would just be smoke with no fire. A eureka moment occurred when I received the wisdom that led me to write this book. I understood that there was no cheating in the marriage, but because of premarital sex, they each planted a seed of doubt in their partners' subconscious minds, and it is now harvesting time.

This seed planted before marriage is simply what gave birth to the paranoia in marriage. Anything in the relationship had the potential to be suspicious about cheating behaviour. One day, a certain husband had a running tummy and spent more time in the restroom. The wife suspected he was chatting with some other females. After executing her own search warrant on his phone, she assumed he had deleted the chats. Before paying attention to the husband's tummy condition, she questioned whose food caused the running stomach, as she was not running if they ate the same food.

Had he known that this would be the result, he would fight to do the right thing for his marriage before the vows. A life of being suspected of cheating by the one you love is no freer than a convicted felon. If you are a suspect or suspicious in your marriage, visit a marriage counsellor before it's too late. If you are not yet married, then do the right thing and you will enjoy the rewards in marriage.

This does not mean that all spouses suspected of cheating have engaged in premarital sex. All it takes to be a suspect is to give a reason to doubt your faithfulness, like hiding information or lack of self-control. Others are suspects not because of what they have done or failed to do, but just because their spouse finds it difficult to trust. Maybe he or she was cheated on before or they are the ones cheating and therefore think everyone else is doing as they do.

Concluding on the sex topic, whatever you have seen in porn movies was just a scripted act for the movie. Do not think you can try that at home, it's nowhere near real-life experiences. Allow actors to be actors and live your reality, being inspired by your own creativity and good morals. The porn movie experience is not relevant to marriage, but only in the porn industry. Unless you aspire to be a porn star, you have no business watching it alone or as a couple.

Chapter 5

Ignoring the prevailing divorce rates

May your marriage never become a divorce statistic! This is my heartfelt prayer for all my readers and all those in marriage or interested in it. I dislike divorce with a passion and do not wish it upon my worst enemies. Divorce is the death of a relationship, more complex than just signing a divorce certificate. The crucial difference between the death of a relationship in divorce and a spouse's death is that divorce has no closure, meaning you can still relive the pain afresh.

The ex-wife or ex-husband is still alive and each time you think or interact with them, the wounds open and bleed again. Each time they look like they are doing well without you feels somehow, any post they make on their status or social media feels personal and all the regrets of disappointment and sacrifices wasted on a person you now think was not worth your time floods your soul.

I heard a sad story recently of a college student whose mother never wants to see her, simply because she looks like her father and reminds the mother of all the past hurts she went through at the hands of her ex-husband. This is sad, but a potential reality in the lives of people affected by a divorce. Apart from the mother's hurt, now another child grows up in rejection, all because of a failed marriage. Listen to me well when I say there is no end to the sorrow caused by divorce.

Divorce is a monster that no one can tame. After encountering this monster, the experience will last for a lifetime. There are no lessons to learn from divorce but from good marriages. I have listened to many divorced people talking of lessons they learned out of the experience. To tell the truth, most of them are not lessons at all but the voice of bitterness and regret while a few have hopeful words. Things like, I have learned not to trust men again, I will not be vulnerable again to anyone, I have learned to be tough and independent, all men are the same, never give all your life to someone, etc… are not marriage advice.

First, I say these are not lessons, but the talk of a hardened heart for future relationships. If these are some of your thoughts, please take time to seek counselling and heal before moving on to another person who will easily become a victim of your past relationship. Also, no one deserves to go through divorce to learn anything. Most times, the person could have learned earlier and avoided divorce, could have learned from other people's divorce cases, and saved their marriage rather than their own experience. It's not worth it.

To show that divorce is a deleterious teacher, past research has shown that second, third, fourth, fifth the divorce rate soars high. I stopped at five because at a point you must stop trying and admit either marriage is not for you, or you are not for marriage. You have a better shot at making it in marriage before divorce than your second and third attempt at it. This is simple: if you have had many failed relationships or marriage in the past, the only common denominator in all those relationships is YOU. At a point, you must stop and introspect.

This introspection is a critical part of every failure or achieving a milestone in any aspect of your life. Sometimes you will find out you are selecting the wrong people or attracting the wrong type for marriage, or you didn't heal from past hurts and you allowing them to spoil your present life, or you will notice an attitude change you need to make before your next attempt or better yet, you will realise you need someone to teach and coach you for marital success.

Sadly, marriage and relationships are the only parts of our lives where people have, accidents, heart breaks, injuries, suffer disabilities, and have relationships end in death, yet no one investigates each case to determine what went wrong, could it have been prevented, whose fault it was, and what can be done to prevent such in the future.

In the aviation industry, at the occurrence of an accident, there is not a stone left unturned by the investigation team, starting from the cockpit conversations (bedroom) to the cabin crew (children), cargo (asserts), passengers (relatives, friends, and colleagues), mechanical failure (love and respect) and fuel (finances), the list goes on even to the control room, air traffic controllers, engineers, and inspectors, etc... Is it not surprising that the aviation industry is more organised than the marriage industry, yet marriage and divorce affects the core of individuals, families, societies, and the nation at large?

Divorce is a reality nowadays. You are very naïve to assume you have natural immunity to it simply because you and your spouse are too special and love each other. There is a way that leads to divorce and a way that leads to bliss in marriage. No matter how much you love each other or how special you think what you have going on is, if you choose the way of divorce, you will surely arrive at the destination.

As a marriage hopeful, you need to understand that a happy marriage is a product of intentional effort. Things do not just flow and fall into pleasant places, but someone must engineer the prosperity, joy, peace, and happiness you wish to see.

A lady approached me for counselling services. I informed her I do not do premarital counselling without the other partner present. During our first session, I sensed some tension and negativity from her partner and unearthed that he was not pro-marriage because everyone closest to him was either divorced, is divorcing or not happy with their marriage. I told him divorce is not a mystery that happens to anyone unexpectedly but a harvest that follows certain seeds planted or weeds and thistle ignored by the couple or one of them. Of course, he did not accept this.

I then gave him a task to go and investigate all the divorced and unhappy marriages he referred to and find out how many books had the spouses bought in the last twelve months on marriage and how many marriage seminars, workshops or conferences had they attended in twelve months. It did not surprise me that his findings shocked him. None of the six people he spoke to had bought books and studiously read them or sought to learn or relearn about marriage in twelve months.

Divorce is a harvest of things you have done or not done as a couple or individual in marriage. The gentleman understood this principle, and I had one question for him; How many books have you bought and read in the last twelve months about your relationship and marriage? With regret, he answered, and I prophesied to him that at his learning pace, his marriage will not outrun divorce. I was happy to see him investing in books and learning about marriage. Few things bring me joy as a counsellor than this, knowing I avoided a future disaster.

Every student enrols for college, knowing fully that others are failing and if they don't work hard, they will also fail. Every employee knows that to stay employed, they must perform or else they will soon receive their dismissal letter. Every entrepreneur knows many startups fail, but they will work hard to not be another statistic. Marriage is the same. Only hard workers, committed, and innovative spouses enjoy the fruits of their labour in marriage.

Marriage alone has no fruits; it is just a field and if left unattended; you get strange and wild plants growing in it and sadly these plants will give you bitter fruits and thorn bushes. In no time you will hear things like, I can't do this anymore, it's not working, I want out; the marriage is irreparable. The field that was full of potential has become a jungle of nightmares. A jungle full of uncertainty, wild unreasonable behaviours and strange and hurtful words thrown around, spite, selfishness, and unforgiveness.

Should the wisdom in this book be appealing to you, you will aim to be an intentional hard worker who tends the field and plants the crops he or she likes. You will joyfully put in the labour, remove weeds, and in due season reap a bountiful harvest of a blissful marriage. If you don't like your harvest, change your seeds, and labour patterns, not the field or owners. Today, you can have a seven-star marriage, one that has no problems and arguments — you have the potential.

What happened to others has a potential to recur in your situation if you use the same formula they used. Not ignoring the reality of divorce will cause two things to happen to you. First, you will choose your marriage partner wisely, and second, you will take matters into your own hands and work hard to build the marriage of your dreams.

The odds are already against you. Studies have shown that up to 50% of marriages end in divorce in at least ten years. How about those who stay married but are not happily married? A dysfunctional family experiences the same adverse effects as a family that has gone through divorce and the impact is the same for children. We are sitting in a scenario where maybe only a smaller than desired percent remain happily married and you need to be one of them by doing things differently.

For you to be one of the good statistics, you need to be very intentional and work hard for your marriage to blossom. Unfortunately, many people today see a happy marriage and desire it. As many do not desire the work that is invested into having one. Every beautiful rose garden has a gardener. The failing of marriages around you is not supposed to deter you from walking down the aisle but to remind you that good marriages don't come cheap.

Be intentional about who feeds you information. Many people today lack excellent mentors and role models for marriage. At a previous company I worked for, some years back, a colleague was having trouble in her marriage. She confided in her female work colleagues. Sadly, the three colleagues were all single mothers, one having divorced and the other two having troubled relationships. They talked her out of her marriage and within eight weeks she moved back to her parent's house.

Not that a divorced single mother does not have good counsel, she just met some who were still bitter about their experiences in past relationships. Whoever feeds you information can determine your marital success or failure.

Had she surrounded herself with people enjoying marriage, she would have received better counsel and learned how to fix her problems than quitting.

Many have failed in marriage, be wise to learn from their mistakes. Do not assume they never loved each other, or they were just unlucky, or they were wrong about each other or were not serious about marriage. The sooner you realise your need to learn, the sooner you will seek to gain wisdom. Do not just marry without fully understanding what will make your marriage a success.

If someone has had it rough in marriage, it doesn't mean that's the nature of marriage, but simply their personal experience was according to their wisdom level. You should mature in knowledge to not see any reason your marriage should be rough or have good and bad days if it is up to you and your spouse to have good, better, and best days.

I often hear people saying in marriage you have ups and downs, some days you will fight and that's ok. Should you have a fight, do not go to bed without resolving the issues. It sounds wise, but wisdom for marriage is strong enough to maintain peace always and prevent fights. Perhaps such are their own experiences, or they have witnessed so many couples fight and concluded it is common. If not, they would offer no one such a caution as advice. I do not relate to a marriage that has fights, arguments or bad days and the same is with all couples I have coached. You can rise above marital problems and only hear marital problems from your neighbours or in the news.

Chapter 6

Premarital counselling is optional.

Many young couples of today feel marital education and coaching are outdated, optional, and for people that have issues in their relationship or failed in their past relationships or marriages. Deception is to think you do not need help when help is your only way to success. Help is best served as a starter than dessert when problems have buffeted you and sucked life out of your relationship to the bone.

Thinking you do not need premarital counselling? I think you have watched too many superhero movies. May I suggest to you that no one is a Superman or Supergirl. We all need some help in one area or the other. Your decision to marry is proof you can't do life alone and need the help of a spouse. The thought that you do not need premarital counselling is like thinking you do not need a trainer and training before a boxing match. The match will be a mismatch to your KO.

Deception is one big cause of many casualties in many young and full of potential lives. While growing up in a ghetto, friends also deceived me and my pride in thinking I could fight and beat Ben. Ben was the new boy in our neighbourhood and my age. I picked a fight with Ben, thinking I would win, and since the mighty Walt had fought many battles and won, I thought it would be a walk in the park and my name initial "W" was synonymous with Winning.

Because of my past success, I assumed I knew how to win. I remember walking to Ben with many witnesses I had gathered singing a victory song, and the fight started. Ben did some new moves on me and somehow, I found myself on the ground feeling dizzy and nose bleeding, and he walked away smartly. It was a brief encounter and a pronounced loss. I stood up and noticed all my friends and supporters had disappeared. Later, I learned Ben was a karate student. The loss to Ben was traumatic to my seven-year-old self, and enough to send me on an early retirement from street fighting.

Most people's experiences in marriage are like my account with Ben. They assume their past pleasant months of relationship success will guarantee marital success. Not knowing you are entering a new territory that you have zilch experience on. A territory with its own new level of challenges and tests. Had someone coached me and told me more about Ben, I would have befriended Ben quickly or sought more time to practise and prepare for the match instead of walking blindly into a certainly mission impossible match.

"You are so cute together", "you are the best couple we have seen", "you are a match made in heaven", etc… are all flattery statements from your friends and family. These are not words of encouragement to get married. Such statements do not have weight in marriage. You may look good together and wear matching clothes, and that does not move a needle to a happy marriage. When Ben was done with me, all my cheerers had deserted me. They were only by my side on good days. The same is with marriage. In your marital success, all your people are there to enjoy with you. However, on the day of trouble, you will be alone with your spouse having silent nights in the bedroom.

I learned very late that Ben should have been a friend, not a foe. You don't have to suffer a loss in marriage to wake up and seek help. You don't have to learn after walking the path of heartaches and divorce. The earlier you gain knowledge, the less humiliating defeats you will encounter in the future.

Each time I hear a couple is getting married, my first question is: did they complete any premarital counselling course? If not, I wonder what magic the couple will use for marriage to work. If it were up to me, I would postpone the wedding until they have invested in their marriage through a course. Everyone needs training and coaching to do well in anything.

I work full time as a commercial manager and often have conversations with the company's Co-Founder and CEO. I am not surprised every time I hear him mention his paid consultants that are coaching him in different areas of his responsibilities. He understands that to perform any critical role, one needs a coach, mentor, and teacher to succeed. His capacity as CEO is the reason the company had the resiliency to prosper against COVID-19 and lockdowns.

You are the Co-Founder and CEO of your marriage. What training have you gained to make your marriage a success? Who is coaching you? Who have you sought after to help you take your marriage to the next level? You stop growing when you stop learning. A rude surprise awaits you in marriage if you think you know it all.

Premarital counselling is not optional or a luxury you can do without. Your vision for a pleasure filled marriage needs strong teaching. A joyful ride till death do you part comes at a cost. Some forgo the premarital counselling for reasons like time. If you cannot make time to prepare healthy meals and exercise, you will make time for doctor visits sooner. One way or the other, you will make time to discuss your marriage, better for premarital counselling than later. Better with a counsellor than time with a divorce lawyer.

What you do not value, you can never allocate time and resources to. Most people underestimate the importance of premarital counselling and the challenges they will face during marriage, which is the reason few people consider it before getting married. Common sense will not solve the challenges you will meet in marriage. You will require depth in wisdom for marriage. Only those who invest in acquiring wisdom can only overcome or avoid marriage obstacles.

Do not flow with the current. Choose to do the right things at the right time and you will reap in due harvest seasons. Should you play in sowing times, you will sulk in harvest time. Choose to be different and secure your marital success.

Part A

Final remarks

If you master the six lessons that I have shared with you, you will have a better shot at prospering in marriage. These six are only a part of laying a solid foundation for your marriage and upon these, you can build your structure. This is your starting point for building your happy marriage. The strength of your marital foundation determines how high your building will go up in marital glory. The quality of materials you will use to build, the furniture and decor that will be in the house and the calibre of visitors you will receive and host in the building.

If your foundation is shaky and suitable for a shack, then do not expect to have a ten-story building with a swimming pool on top. There is furniture in this world that will never enter a shack, moving staircases from one story of a building to the next are an impossibility for your building.

There are some people in life whom you will never invite or honour your invite to a shack.

The best time to dream and design the marriage you want is before the marriage. Use all your courtship days to lay a solid foundation for your desired marriage tomorrow. Overcoming these six deceptions is a major victory worthy of being celebrated in your marital preparation phase.

The foundation phase has a lot of sweating and sacrifices, but all are worth it for the glorious future you wish to have. It will be a sacrifice for you to stop cohabiting, to stop having sex and to pay for counselling services, but it will all be worth it. You will thank me later.

I have seen no one build a firm foundation and not proceed to building the walls, roof, and other necessary parts of the building. Surely you cannot just abstain from sex and assume you will now have marital success. No! Many have led successful platonic relationships and forgot the other elements necessary for the marriage to work. The foundation is critical. It has a start and finish date. The foundation phase starts the day both of you acknowledge the relationship and ends on the altar, making way for the next phase of building the structure all the way to furnishing the complete building.

Working for your marriage does not end at the wedding. When the minister is officiating your wedding, he or she is officiating you into the work of marriage. This is a continuous process, however, just like in the construction industry, every high-rise building requires heavy machinery and a lot of hard work for the foundation and thereafter the work becomes lighter and easier. Pay the price before the vows and play later in marriage. It's better than to play before the vows and pay a hard price in marriage.

Part B

The case for premarital counselling

Part B

Introduction

Part B of this book will explore the best strategy for marital readiness. I will do my best to show you critical reasons for premarital counselling. It should be compulsory for every couple before issuing a marriage licence.

Think of your life five decades from today. Will your fashion style for today matter? Will you treasure the hairstyle, branded wear, the car you drove? What do you think will matter to you the most at seventy, at eighty, or at ninety years of life on earth? You will agree with me, you would have forgotten the clothes you wore ten years ago, but people who affected your life you have engraved in your memory.

What truly matters in life are not the possessions that we have, the bank account balance and investments, but the relationships we have built, lives we have affected, and lessons learned along the way. Deep down, you know this is true, right? Yet you allow yourself to be distracted by vain time wasters while we take important relationships for granted.

Many people get caught up in the web of chasing after material gains and inevitably set themselves up for regret later in marriage. I have seen many successful middle-aged professionals who have no one to spend their money and enjoy their possessions with after a failed marriage and family life. These midlife folks easily fall prey to online romance scams and losing their hard-earned money trying to gain love and companionship. Pursue a gainful career, a startup venture, and your dreams, but not at the expense of your marriage and relationships.

One relationship you will cherish till death is your marriage. We normally expect to bury our parents, and not the opposite, and your only close relation will be your spouse in the later years of your life. Of course, you have friends and siblings. These are with you while your spouse is present for you. Friends and siblings will pursue opportunities elsewhere and move to other cities and countries, but your spouse will always be with you wherever you go.

The older you grow, the clearer your perspective of life becomes. Life will humble you gradually. With ageing, you will realise people are the greatest treasure you could have with you. A complete shift of mind from youth and young adults who think they can do without people and give up on every relationship too easily. Majority of depressed and hurting people normally have no one by their side to share their life experiences with.

Do your best and give all you can to your marriage. It starts with premarital preparations. Martin and Martin (1984) advises there is a need for premarital counselling and communication programs for engaged couples to improve their relationships and increase their chances for marital satisfaction. This section is dedicated to exploring premarital counselling.

Chapter 7

Premarital counselling prevents future problems.

Premarital counselling concludes before the wedding day, by the wedding date, each couple should have amassed enough knowledge to start and grow a family. In my time in counselling couples, I have learned that prevention is better than cure. Couples who completed a premarital counselling course before marriage have better marriages compared to couples that did not.

In health terms, the cost of disease prevention is lower than the cost of curing a disease. The cost of avoiding and preventing marital problems does not compare to the cost of a broken-down marriage and trying to fix it. With our ever-progressive medical technology, we are yet to produce a cure for HIV/AIDS and by the time we secure a cure, we can safely assume it will be very expensive for an average citizen without medical insurance. It is not surprising that over five decades later, since the first case of HIV/AIDS we have no cure, but preventative methods and measures were long tried and proved to be effective. Sexual health professionals simply advise either to abstain from sex or to use a condom as the best methods of preventing HIV/AIDS.

HIV-1 infection in human blood was first detected in 1959 in a blood sample taken from a dead man in Kinshasa. In the year of the first HIV/AIDS diagnosis, condoms were already on the market. During those times, condoms were primarily used to prevent a few known infections and pregnancy. In 1844, vulcanization of rubber led to the production of cheap condoms, which was then improved with latex in 1930. More improvements in the following years led to more comfortable, scented and sophisticated condom production.

The invention of condoms before the discovery of HIV/AIDS clearly shows us that prevention is our best chance to stay out of trouble. Let us say Tom is a promiscuous young adult, should he contract the virus, he will enrol into a life of medication and doctor visits to manage the virus which is high-priced compared to the cost of buying and using condoms or better yet abstaining.

Premarital counselling is a preventative measure of future problems in marriage. It is worth the investment more than the cost of managing marital problems. Your relationship is better and beautiful when you learn to prevent problems than seeking to fix relationship problems. The solution to preventing future marital problems is already available in the form and shape of premarital counselling. It is wisdom to seek not to learn by your own experiences, hence I strongly recommend that you act today and seek to learn from others before you tie the knot.

Edwin S Soji, said, "every relationship is like glass made up of trust and love, once it breaks, the reflection won't be the same again". Of course, relationships can be restored, and I am a firm believer. I do it all the time. If a relationship has broken down or trust broken, it will not be the same again as if nothing happened. If the couple works hard towards restoration, they can learn from it and have an even better marriage after and if they do not work hard, the opposite will be true. The beauty of premarital counselling is in making sure that the glass of love and trust never breaks.

One topic I teach couples on my premarital counselling course is infidelity, which is a common cause of divorce. Once infidelity creeps into a marriage, it usually proves arduous to deal with and overcome for most couples. I address this topic and equip the couple simply with a goal to leave no room for future extra-marital affairs. It is unwise to assume people know how to avoid and uphold faithfulness to one partner. In this era of increasing influence from the liberalism movement coupled with the sexual revolution, couples have to put more effort and boundaries to stay faithful.

I have met women who now accept that men cheat and such is not out of the normal. Though it is an unpleasant topic for fiancé's who are planning to marry, we all can't ignore and pretend it is a nonfactor. As much as we emphasis on communication, finances, and other topics, we also should explore sex and its glorious potentials without ignoring the destructive nature of sex outside marriage, its consequences, and a sure proof way to prevent it.

Please note, "prevent" means to keep or restrain something from happening or existing at all, to make it impossible. This is the full potential that premarital counselling holds. It has a capacity to keep your marriage from quarrels, fights, unmet expectations, arguments, and divorce. With marital happiness at stake, no one has the luxury to assume or ignore premarital counselling.

Problems in marriage are like a wildfire, they are extinguished if dealt with while they start and are smaller than when the fire has spread, and the entire forest is burning. The difference between a fire and a wildfire is the controllable nature of fire and the wildness of the other. During courtship, you have the opportunity to identify and put out small fires before they become wildfires in marriage. Marriage has an amplifying effect on courtship. If you had a healthy relationship and prepared well whilst in courtship, the same will be amplified. A relationship that had ups and downs, fights and arguments, less trust and confusion will be amplified in marriage should the couple not invest in premarital counselling.

I normally highlight to married couples that any behaviour or attitude you dislike in your spouse you probably saw before marriage but expected it to disappear like phantoms. It may have been possible to uncover and resolve some of these problems long before the wedding if premarital counselling had been given its due.

Premarital counselling avoids honest mistakes that are costly. There are mistakes I call honest mistakes in relationships and marriage. This is when you thought you were doing the right thing to fix a problem, but it results in creating more trouble or hurt for yourself, your spouse, or your relationship. The difference between a foolish mistake and an honest mistake is intent. You intended your actions or words for good, but in error, you executed. Had you known the consequences earlier, you would not choose the same. A foolish mistake has wrong intentions and usually the results of such are known. Wrong intentions are to cause trouble, hurt, or disappointment.

An example of a foolish mistake is revenge because your partner did or said something wrong or hurtful and you do a wrong so you can be even. I have seen many cases of revenge cheating both in relationships and in marriage. Simply because your partner cheated does not justify your cheating, so your partner can feel the same pain. Foolish wisdom in marriage is to think you give your spouse only what they deserve or acting and speaking like a judge who hands down punishments for wrongs done and rewards no good.

Premarital counselling will give you wisdom on how to relate to each other and avoid such foolish mistakes. Premarital counselling will teach you that there is no fifty-fifty in marriage. You do your hundred and your spouse does their hundred and you each have hundred. Your spouse's failure to give a hundred is no wise indicator to give less. Giving less will ensure gradual deterioration of the quality of your marriage. If you continue to outperform, your partner will soon learn and desire to reciprocate the best for you.

The sense of "I will not because my spouse hasn't" has no wisdom to it. It has been your pleasure to do many things for many others, expecting nothing in return. Your spouse deserves even more. There is no place for tit-for-tat in marriage and it is more appropriate for children. It is imperative to know that foolish mistakes will only lead to hurting your spouse and yourself. Any revenge on your spouse hurts you more because they have become a significant part of you.

Premarital counselling will help you avoid such foolish and intentional mistakes, therefore saving your marriage from future hurt and failure. One of my favourite reality TV shows, Paternity court, presided over by Judge Lauren Lake, has proved the failure of tit-for-tat in relationships. I always watch on the show that ladies who have cheated because the husband cheated end up with paternity doubt in their cup. Imagine telling your husband, "Honey, we are pregnant" with excitement and his response is like, "Who is the father?" or "I want a DNA test". Instead of celebrations, you receive a special moment spoiler.

Not that the husband is justified in the cheating, but your actions did not solve his cheating and created a paternity problem. I have also learned that men who cheated on their spouses struggled to have great relationships with their children in the future. The unintended consequences of their actions would be long lasting.

I don't know about you, but I would rather have one problem to work on than two complicated problems. Wrong behaviour often has a way of producing ripple consequences. Surely cheating does not resolve a cheating problem.

Honest mistakes are more common in romantic relationships than intentional foolish mistakes. Sadly, honest mistakes also have consequences and can be costly. You are marrying or married to a human being with a capacity to err, leave room for error until you reach heaven. Honest mistakes are avoidable, or their consequences can be mitigated simply by acquiring wisdom. Honest mistakes are a product of not knowing the best way to handle situations or being miss informed.

In a zoom counselling session with a couple in another city, the wife realised that the way she was talking to her husband discouraged him from helping with house chores. She would say things like, "real men do dishes", "other husbands clean after themselves" and the husband had no interest as he felt pressure to add up to other man or prove he was a real man. She quickly changed and started saying things like "I felt your love and appreciation yesterday when you did dishes", "Thank you for helping with trash, I am happy you support me with house chores". In no time, the husband was doing more because she began focusing on the small things he was doing right and appreciating them.

The lady had no intention to discourage, rather to motivate him to do more, but in a wrong way that resulted in the opposite of what she wanted. In receiving new information in counselling, you learn to deal with issues and avoid them in the future.

I listened to a young man complaining why his wife could not be happy with them staying with his parents and kept bringing the issue up. They had moved in with his family to save on costs and prepare to buy their own house; it made sense. This was an honest mistake as they intended to save money for their own house but ignored the dynamics of staying with in-laws, especially in your early days of marriage, while learning to be in the same environment with your spouse.

His wife was not happy that all their decisions were not their own decisions as the family kept on interfering. She had no privacy, and they could not just go out with the two of them for dinner. Had they gone through premarital counselling, they would have learned wisdom to manage in-law relationships and that saving money while losing marital happiness is not a worth trade off. I have seen marriages crumble simply because of the influence of family and friends. You can avoid such problems by educating yourself prior to marriage.

Premarital counselling will bring clarity and define things for your marriage. There is no tricky field to play in than one that has no clearly defined terms. Having clarity about why things must be done a certain way is essential to a successful marriage. This clarity includes clarity on priorities, clarity on purpose, and how to live with and love each other. Do not enter marriage with unsolved mysteries. You cannot allow your marriage to be a mystery movie. I have encountered many young, even mature people who think love is so mysterious to define and understand. This is far from the truth. The more you understand love, the more you will have a simplified and happy marriage. Seek clarity of everything before you sign the papers.

Chapter 8

Premarital counselling increases your chances of marital bliss.

Researcher's Stanley, Amato, Johnson and Markman published in the Journal of Family Psychology (April 2006) findings from research titled; Premarital education, marital quality, and marital stability: Findings from a large, random household survey. One of their key findings showed couples that completed premarital counselling were 31% happier and more satisfied in marriage than couples who did not go through counselling. This means the couples who completed premarital counselling are 31% less likely to divorce than those who did not.

I do not know about you but to me 31% is too much to ignore. Shark tank, one of my favourite TV shows, broadcasts real investment discussions between an entrepreneur and a panel of investors. I have watched many negotiations end with no deals because the investor and entrepreneur could not agree on 1% equity in a company. In equities, 51% means you own the business while the other with 49% is called a minority shareholder. That 1% determines who makes strategic decisions in the business and losing it means you have lost control of the business.

I do not think the value of 1% in marital happiness and a less likelihood of divorce is less vital than the 1% in equity ownership of a company. Every 1% in marriage is worth fighting for and worth spending sleepless nights and your dollars just to gain more percentages of happiness and satisfaction in marriage. The research study discovered a 31% difference in favour of couples who valued premarital counselling versus those who did not. We can explain this as follows; couples who do not invest in premarital counselling can only achieve a maximum of 69% satisfaction and happiness in marriage. In college terms, this means your marriage can never be a pass with distinction, you will have an average to poor marriage.

To expound the seriousness of this research's findings, I suggest to you that couples that completed premarital counselling are 31% less likely to divorce than couples who did not. Counselling does not guarantee marital success but increases the chances with 31%. Statistically, in the USA, every couple on their wedding day has a 50-50 chance to divorce or not. A 50% probability applies for the USA. For your country, please research and find out the statistics.

If you have a 50% divorce probability and you add premarital counselling, then your chance of divorce drastically reduces to 19% while the probability of marital success rises to 81% which is a distinction and 81% to 19% are good odds to place a bat against.

There is no downside to premarital counselling, as much as there is no disadvantage in acquiring new helpful knowledge. Anyone who invests in premarital counselling stands to benefit and reap the rewards thereof, such as a problem free marriage. Premarital counselling is a learning program where you are taught and prepared for what is coming. The reason premarital counselling translates to increased fulfilment in marriage is because it shapes your thinking, attitudes, understanding, expectations, and intentions into being auspicious for an enjoyable marital life.

My mentor always says harvest follows a seed, not a need, so many people desire to harvest the beautiful fruits of marriage while they skipped the seed sowing time. Marital bliss is a harvest, one that comes after a season of planting and labouring. If you labour now, you will surely reap the fruit of your hard work, but if you downplay the sowing season, you will certainly envy those who invested in premarital counselling when they are enjoying their marriages. Your labour in premarital counselling increases your joy in marriage.

Premarital counselling improves conflict resolution, negotiation, and communication skills while increasing relationship quality and satisfaction. Majority of marriage problems are communication related. The problems range from the exchange of diverging or opposite views, typically in a heated or angry way, to no words at all. Besides marriage, communication problems can also occur between the couple and extended family members, friends, and children.

Other couples struggle with having hard conversations. Conversations like raising issues of concern while those who can raise the issues do so with a wrong approach. With communication problems prevented through premarital counselling, you have a good probability of enjoying marriage success.

Chapter 9

Premarital counselling uncovers relationship blind spots.

Love carries with it powerful emotions. When someone finds love, it's like the dawn of a new era of their life filled with happiness, joy, laughter, anticipation, and splendid memories. Love is powerful enough to change a person's routine, lifestyle, career, city of residence, and religion. You will think about your partner when you make small and big decisions in a relationship, and more so in marriage.

Sometimes love birds make these decisions consciously thinking about their partner and sometimes they unconsciously decide thinking they are making the right choices. The nature of love makes it easy for the glorious moments shared in a relationship to cloud your reasoning on red flags and water down unresolved issues, recurring issues, and challenges.

Premarital counselling brings a third and unbiased eye into your relationship, an eye with no blurry vision on all aspects of the relationship and free from the emotional connection you have with your partner. Your counsellor knows how to identify red flags and how to bring them to your attention in a manner you will fully understand why the concerns are not to be overlooked and map a strategy on how to fix the issue before marriage.

I will talk more about the counsellor later, but for now, it is important to know your counsellor can advise, suggest, strongly recommend, and help you move your relationship to a better place. It is not up to your counsellor to decide for you. Instead, they present options with recommendations, consequences, and rewards associated with each choice. Regardless, the decision is yours to make, and its consequences are also yours to enjoy.

On one of the "Hey Steve" shows, Steve Harvey said "do not get into a habit of collecting red flags", as he gave advice to a young lady. He said it very well, and that is why I follow his shows. Love birds often ignore red flags such as poor communication, traits of abuse, ungratefulness, integrity, honesty, keeping secrets, lies, friends or relatives with bad influence on the relationship.

How sad. Ignoring red flags is like ignoring a red traffic light and crossing your fingers that nothing bad happens. You may get away with one, but surely this is a formula for suicide. Should you survive the accident, you may become disabled or come out with scars. The same with relationships, red flags are not to be ignored but uprooted and dealt with decisively to avoid headaches in the future.

I have seen partners who cannot question their beloved's spending patterns, relations with the opposite sex, friends with bad influence, alcohol abuse, can't hold a job, and live in an untidy space. If they can't keep their place clean, you can expect your living space to be the same and you will have to commit to a life of cleaning after them. If they can't hold a job, you will be the back-up plan for them, whenever they quit or get fired. Bad friends, indecent relations, or poor financial decision patterns will not disappear because you walked down the aisle. Rather, marriage will amplify these.

If you are not happy with their drinking habits currently, chances are they may not cease, or even become worse in marriage. If funds in their bank accounts are exhausted a week or two after or away from the next pay-check, you may sign up for such a life. Despite the wedding, if your partner has a tendency to flirt with other girls or boys, expect such behaviour even after the ceremony. If their close friends are cheating on their partners, chances are you are next or you just haven't caught them.

No one in marriage aspires to be stuck with any of the above cases, though before marriage you may tolerate them, but in marriage, they will be a thorn in your flesh, and you won't be silent about them. If you won't be silent tomorrow about them, rather start today to sound the alarm and get help. Rather cry today than save your cry for tomorrow. If you choose to not turn a blind eye to these issues, you will deal with a cub and win, but in marriage the cub will strengthen to a decorated and masculine male lion, monstrous enough to see you out of marriage.

If you wait until marriage, they will marry and are happy you love them as they are. I have seen the statement "I want someone to love me as I am" being misused and used for blackmail in relationships. "Why can't you love me as I am?" People love you as you are but also expect you to become a better person for the future we want together. Surely you can't be the same person in a different future, so your spouse must be a willing spouse to become a better person because they love you, too.

Should you attempt to solve red flags and you see a deep-seated unwillingness to make adjustments, then this is the sign you needed? The sign telling you if they are the one for you or not. Choosing to marry them would be to marry a version 1.0 problem, but with title upgrades and a wedding ring, you will have version 5.2 problem. More sophisticated to deal with that, even your ancestors will marvel.

Your spouse will not be happy with you raising problems of issues you have been ok with in the past. They will feel cheated instead of seeing their need to change. They will wonder why you now want them to change. I think they are justified in this trend of thought; it is like if you knew before they married you they had a child, then why should that child now bother you in marriage? What you did not confront before the vows has a right to remain in marriage. Your silence communicated your approval, thus according to your partner's understanding.

Is love blind? Such a question has led to a TV show premiered in 2020 on Netflix trying to provide answers in a social reality TV experiment. In the last episode of the first season, the producers suggested it could be blind. I think love is not blind, but the person in love can turn a blind eye to certain faults and issues. Love is a beautiful and perfect thing that has no weakness or error in it, but how you manage it can be your weakness and error and blindness is one of them.

Have you ever tried to tell a friend that their relationship is bad for them? Chances are if you have done it in the past, you are no longer friends with the person or, at most, your friendship is no longer close as before this type of conversation. The only reason they did not listen to you is not because you were a bad person trying to destroy their relationship, but they simply did not see things the same way as you do. They were blinded from seeing things from your perspective.

What you thought was a problem, to them, it was immaterial because of differing viewpoints. The reality is you are not onboard their love flight and on the ground. Where you are standing, a mountain is a problem, but up in the plane, they do not see why it should be a concern to you. My pastor always says that there are three people difficult to convince otherwise in life and one of them is a damsel in love.

I have many stories to share about this, but I will share about Charlie. Charlie was a church boy. He grew up in church, had followed the advice of his pastor and parents growing up and became a successful young man. He had a good job and was talented in music. After a few songs were released, he was growing in popularity and one day he saw a beautiful sister in the church congregation and his love story began. The first time Charlie went against his parents and pastor was on this matter. He felt like they had controlled him enough and it was time for him to make his own decisions with no advice from others.

The only issue raised was that no one knew this girl and Charlie was falling too fast in love towards the altar and skipped premarital counselling. Only after the vows, Charlie learned the girl had lied about her past and had a child from her past relationship. This, to his surprise. Because of the frustration, Charlie's wife fell back to her past life of alcoholism and a few more blows later led to divorce.

Charlie lived in my childhood neighbourhood. He passed on in my high school days and we buried all the future potentials he had with him. A cousin of mine said something powerful. All the signs were there. It was just too good to be true, and we knew it, but the last person to realise it was Charlie. You only have one future and marriage has the capacity to bury all your potential. Be awake and seek to have no blind spots. You cannot afford to marry only knowing what they wanted you to hear.

With your eyes open, you can spot any red flags and with your mind sober, you can direct yourself with wisdom. Premarital counselling has a way to uproot all areas you are turning a blind eye on; you should be prepared to invest anything just for you to see the accurate picture of your relationship.

In our generation, people have learned the art of pretending, living a different life from the one they show everyone else. I have seen people going to expensive hotels under the guise of viewing for future business, taking photos and posting as if they spent money to be at the hotel. This is sad. Why not work hard and afford yourself a night in some fancy place, then you can take pictures for yourself, not for the public to see but for your own memories? There are some behaviours you would not see royalty do. Treat yourself as royalty.

I have heard countless stories of people who liked someone on social media and only to realise they have two lives, one for the internet and one for the home. Unfortunately, marriage is not an internet sensation but is a home-based practice. Desire to understand the real person behind the pictures and the stories they are telling you. Even if they can fool you, it is almost impossible for them to fool a seasoned marriage counsellor. Premarital counselling can add a safety net for you should you be about to marry a pretender.

I recently watched a Tyler Perry movie titled "A Fall from Grace" and Shannon DeLong successfully pretended to be the perfect husband that Grace Waters never had. Only after the vows, he stopped opening the car door, serving breakfast in bed, late dinner dates and all other romantic gestures. Not only did he stop the good, but defrauded Grace of her life savings, destroyed her career and set her up for murder with a life sentence in prison.

Grace admitted she saw the signs, but ignored them. She felt it was too good to be true, but enjoyed the ride. See, when someone is in love, they tend to dismiss their mind and ride on the wave of gifts and romantic gestures. She wanted it so badly that she hastened the marriage, fearing she would lose him. Anything done from a position of fear in a love relationship is like using a medical plaster or band-aid on a broken bone. You cannot marry because you are afraid to lose them. You cannot bear someone as a child because you are afraid of losing them. You cannot have sex with them because you are afraid they will end the relationship. Anything done in fear simply prolongs or delays the inevitable loss.

Be careful not to fall into the same trap as Grace Waters did. Had grace read the signs, she would have run for her life. She never saw where he stayed, who he lived with, gladly accepted the story that he was an orphan. He would be with her until 02:00am the following day. No hard-working man can afford to see their beloved for 8 hours a day after work and going to work the following day. I can go on and on about how many red flags Grace Waters did not see or ignored in the moment's glee, but the most important one is that there was no premarital counselling. Their relationship started and ended with just the two of them.

There is a rise in romance scams in developed nations. 60 Minutes Australia produced a documentary in 2019 published on their YouTube channel. The documentary shows an investigation of a woman who was scammed of her life savings in the name of love, a solemn promise of marriage and a happily ever after tale. On a list of plus eighty contacts on the scammer's phone, they found a strike rate of almost 100% and they deduced that all the scammed women had one common attribute–desperation for love and companionship.

They may not scam you of anything material, like money or assets, but the cost of a shadow relationship, saturated with shadowy behaviours, can leave you at a point of no return. It is because of such relationships that many are giving up hope for their marital dreams. The emotional stress and quantity of time wasted is too costly for someone with only one life.

The statement "It is better to die trying" does not apply to relationships, especially before marriage. Do not let your desperation for love and companionship or just to have someone sending you good morning texts cloud your voice of reason, to your detriment. Never be too desperate to settle for less than what you deserve. In matters of love, desperate people do desperate and foolish things. The more desperate you are for love, is the more you make regrettable mistakes. It is wisdom never to be so desperate.

To a hungry person, every bitter thing can be sweet. Do not make lifetime decisions for a moment or sense of pleasure. More often than not, desperate people in relationships are taken advantage of. Desperate lovers are more prone to abuse because desperation increases their tolerance level for unacceptable relationship behaviours.

Some desperation even comes from peer pressure. Not that your peers are coercing you, but simply because most are now married or in stable relationships and feel your own pressure to level up. There is no hurry to marry, it's neither a race nor a competition. Be comfortable writing your own unique love life story rather than imitating your peers. The beauty of life is in our differences. God created it that way.

Do not succumb to pressure to marry from relatives. This is more common in Africa. Aunties and uncles may be a pester to you but be in control of your destiny choices and seasons. If you are old enough to marry in their sight, they should also understand you are mature enough to choose your progress and allow you some space.

Uncovering relationship blind spots will avoid future marital shocks. I know many people like romantic surprises as a gesture of effort and thoughtfulness. There are surprises that no one appreciates to be revealed, especially after the wedding, the shocking type of surprises. Premarital counselling will be thorough and help you avoid most of these surprises. The effect of dangerous surprises in marriage is akin to losing a limb. Avoid such at all costs.

Sometimes the issue is not blind spots, some couples have just not matured their communication to discuss anything and everything, including critical but constructive conversations. Subjects like getting an HIV test, any knowledge of STDs, meddling close relatives, finances, respect, boundaries, and many others are not a common or easy discussion for couples. Premarital counselling will leave no stone unturned on any of these issues, helping you discuss and resolve them before they become complex in marriage.

In conclusion, I say, having blind spots in a relationship is like fetching water with a leaking vessel. It's a losing battle. When you get to marriage, you will realise you have carried an empty jar of happiness. If something comes back to bite you, it will become a bigger problem in the future because you have not dealt with it. I implore you to do something now and address all your issues and seek to discover any that you have missed.

Chapter 10

Premarital counselling brings a sense of direction.

Nothing is more aggravating for a woman than being in an uncertain relationship and loving someone who she is not sure wants a future with her. One Saturday at noon, I received an urgent request for a counselling session from Elizabeth. I advised her to make time with her partner and have an online session as they stay in another city. Her partner missed the meeting, and I heard her out. Liz did not beat about the bush; she was clear that she wanted marriage, but after five years of courtship with no sign of a proposal, she was tired.

Several scenarios ran through my mind. If she was my sister, I would man-handle her out of the relationship. The man she was with was a wicked man. How can he be a good man and not say anything about marriage after five years of courtship? The last scenario had more wisdom, and that informed my approach. This was more on empathy for both Liz and for her partner. No sane human can be loyal in a relationship for five years with one person and not desire to marry them. Something must be holding them back or the fear of something serious enough to hold fort for so long.

When I finally met Liz's partner, he was open enough to reveal his disappointments from the divorce experiences of family, relatives, and friends that he witnessed. I knew all he needed was some time to go through a counselling course that would put an end to their journey of wandering in the wilderness of singlehood.

Purpose and direction are more critical in life than effort, misdirected efforts get you nowhere and accomplish nothing meaningful. In relationships, direction is more important than speed, as direction determines destination. It is better to have a clear path of direction and destination in a relationship to avoid wandering unnecessarily.

Goals determine direction and pace. Every relationship should have goals and milestones to measure progress. The milestones do not have to be big but for singles could be things like family introductions, books to be read, savings for dowry (if applicable), a wedding date, etc. while for married couple's things like children, savings, and investments, holidays, buying a family home, and many more make up a good list of milestones.

I have met many young couples, and it is not surprising that many in relationships do not have goals they are working towards. I even had a case of an eight-year-old relationship with no wedding date insight. Your premarital counsellor will help you set clear and achievable timelines, as their interest in you is to see you grow into marriage and live your full potential.

The longer you take to have a sense of direction, is the longer you take wandering in the wilderness in circles. Starting your premarital counselling sessions is a major milestone in courtship, as it shows that you are both on the same page and progressing intentionally. When all the challenges and misunderstandings you have been facing are eliminated, you will easily plan in one direction.

It does not take you more than a year to decide to marry this person or not. Courtship is mainly to get you to this decision, and you will have your entire lives to study and know each other. It is incorrect to still be trying to know a person for over a year without a firm decision to marry. Even when you are married, you will realise you can never learn and finish learning from your spouse. Premarital counselling helps you get to this understanding.

Broken and failed relationships resemble time wasted. Think of it, how do you feel after spending five years with a person with hopes to marry and the dream fades away as the relationship breaks? Five years all gone into the drain; whatever lessons you came out with did not require you to learn them in five years. In five years, you can complete an undergraduate, honours, and masters' qualifications in some study fields. That's too much time to be in a relationship.

Premarital counselling helps largely with marital readiness, by boosting your confidence that the two of you have what it takes to make marriage work. The more confident you are about your relationship, the earlier you will decide to tie the knot. During the courtship phase, a wedding date is a good sense of direction.

Signs that your relationship lacks direction:

1.   When you have never discussed getting married to each other and you are not comfortable to start the conversation. The reason for courtship is to get married. If your man has not brought this topic within the first six months of the relationship, then he may not be thinking of marriage with you. As a lady, you should be able

to bring this topic up for discussion because you are a partner in the project.

2. When you often makeup and break up. A relationship is not like a light bulb, it does not have a switch to turn on and off. It is called a breakup because you are breaking something never meant for breaking. Each time you make up and break up, you grow familiar and easily can do it again. Breaking up means you both lacked the wisdom to make your relationship work. Making up is not solving the reason you broke up, and your time apart does not solve your problems.

If you pay attention, you notice that people who breakup and makeup, will repeat the same until they are tired of making up again. It's simply because they love each other but lack wisdom on how to remain with each other. If you are in this type of relationship, I recommend you walk out and never return, as you will not get to the altar. If you do, your marriage with this person will be like a suspense drama to those around you as you continue the cycle of breaking up and making up.

3. When you are always arguing. There is nothing good about arguing as a couple, rather it's a sign of weak communication skills or strategy from both of you. People or couples disagree all the time. Everyone is entitled to a different opinion. An argument is an exchange of opposing views, but in an angry manner or heated environment.

In an argument, your goal is to show why your position is superior, and your opponent should drop theirs by use of verbal force. A simple escalation from this you have physical force. Arguments are toxic in relationships, you are better alone than in a quarrelsome relationship.

It is better to dwell in the wilderness than with a contentious and angry spouse. I have a distant relative who used to breakup and makeup with his girlfriend. Disregarding every relatives' advice, they got married and had three children. They never stopped the breaking and making even after getting married. Their fate was sealed.

They divorced just seven years into marriage. Lack of direction in a relationship translates to lack of direction in marriage.

4.   When you are not earning money. You will need money to marry, stay married and to take care of your children. A relationship with the two of you not earning means you cannot plan and execute any marital plans.

5.   When there is a lack of trust. Trust is critical for any form of relationship and more so for a couple. It is impossible for anyone to marry someone they cannot trust. Without trust, your relationship lacks direction.

A relationship may have the above signs and still result in marriage. It means the relationship had a good sense of a wrong direction. You should have changed direction and head back to singlehood and not to continue to marry. Your delayed decision averts a breakup but not a divorce. Remember, your goal is not to be married but to be happily married and never divorce. What use is it to marry in January and divorce in December of the same year?

Part C

Marital readiness

Part C

Introduction.

How do I know I am ready for marriage? When is the right time to marry? I do not think my partner is ready for marriage. Had we learned early about marriage, our early days would have been less rough. We learned marriage the hard way, by experience. All these are the common statements I am used to hearing as couples narrate their love stories.

What if I tell you, you can lay all your questions to rest and start having answers? What if I tell you, it is not everyone who is having a rough start in marriage? What if I tell you there are people who have learned to prolong their honeymoon weekend to a honeymoon life? I must tell you; happy marriages are a product of design, not chance or circumstances.

Some have designed a marriage that never experiences intermittent happiness. It is not uncommon for some couples to design a marriage unconsciously with sporadic moments of happiness and episodes of bad vibes. Some couples strive for perpetual happiness and joy in their marriage, while others are accustomed to the ups and downs of their love relationship. Your marital experiences are a product of your creation. Unless you are in a forced marriage, your marital situation will be a product of your choices.

Through marital readiness and wisdom, you become a master of your marital fate. There is no better place to learn and prepare for marriage than in a premarital training or counselling program. If success in marriage is by luck, then readiness and wisdom are the parents of luck.

In the upcoming chapters, I will delve more into the technical details on marital preparation.

Chapter 11

What topics should constitute a standard premarital counselling program.

Marriage is a global institution. Its foundations are universal in India, China, USA, Russia, Thailand, Botswana, Canada, Zimbabwe, and every other country you may think of from small to big. The principles that govern the marriage union are universal to humanity and such principles ought to be explored during a standard premarital counselling session. Principles like love, loyalty, respect, intimacy, communication, exclusivity, sacrifice, and others distinguish the marital relationship from all other forms of relationships that exist within the realm of human relations.

In layperson's terms, premarital counselling is simply preparation for marriage, and this should encompass at the very least all the basics of a marital relationship. This period should bring you to a comprehensive understanding of what marriage really is and what it will take to make your marriage work in its uniqueness. I had a conversation with a young lady who had married early and got divorced. She thought the primary reason for the divorce was marrying just after her 21st birthday, which she thought was too early.

She said at twenty-one years old she did not know how to be a wife and manage a marriage. I suggested to her that age was not the problem, but what she did not know caused her divorce, not the age. I proposed to her, had she married at forty years old, still not knowing or assuming she knows what makes marriage work, she would still get the same results.

A standard premarital counselling should be good enough to equip every aspiring amateur with enough knowledge, wisdom and understanding to make their marriage work in all seasons. A good counselling program must exhaustively discuss the following four aspects:

1.   **Communication**
   - How communication will strengthen or destroy a marriage.
   - How to communicate through conflict, and constructive conversations.
   - How to communicate in a challenging environment, raise issues, de-escalate issues and negotiation.

- How technology can destroy or build a marriage.

2. **Marital foundations**

    - How to be a great wife to your husband.

    - How to be a great husband to your wife.

    - How to nature and grow love in marriage.

    - How to respect and love your spouses.

    - How to gain wisdom, knowledge and understanding for marriage continually.

    - Transitioning from single to spouse and how to deal with change in marriage.

3. **Family operations**

    - How to manage family finances and value systems.

    - How to make family decisions and create a family culture.

    - How to manage extended relationships and start a family.

    - How to manage home responsibilities and duties.

- Understanding divorce and how to stay happily married.

4. **Bedroom matters**

- Sex for beginners and how to keep the fire burning.
- Infidelity, trust, and honesty.
- The wedding and honeymoon.

The above is simply an outline of some basics that should be covered, not a blueprint but a guideline of subjects you will need to become knowledgeable about before the wedding day. As you prepare for your marriage, do not leave any of the subjects above to guess work.

Should your premarital counselling course not go to the depths you need, I suggest you seek knowledge from books and have extensive discussions with your partner to build wisdom in those areas.

Chapter 12

Timing is everything.

The "when" of counselling is as important as the quality of counsel you will receive. Timing is everything. An athlete understands the value of a millisecond, and a pregnant mother who gave birth to a premature baby comprehends the value of a month. There are two sayings I love about time. The first one says, "the early bird catches the worm" and the second one goes like "the second mouse gets the cheese".

Your counselling can not be haphazard. I have seen a trend with couples that is saddening, where couples only seek counselling after experiencing problems. I subscribe to the thought that problems are a late sign that you need counselling. An early sign is when things are good. Counselling offered in good times prevents bad times. In your happy days, seek counselling. Such yields more results than when in trouble.

Melissa and Ryan narrated their love story in my office. I picked the sense that Melissa was growing too familiar with Ryan's presence in her life and was entertaining a habit of complaining. I helped her correct her perspective and their relationship was on a growth trajectory again. Ryan had never brought it up as an issue, but I know from experience that such behaviour would become a thorn in their relationship.

Timing is critical, enrol for a premarital counselling course sooner than later. I normally recommend couples to start as early as three months into their relationship. Premarital counselling done timeously will make your journey to marriage a joy ride. Marriage counselling done timeously will prevent or cure the cancer at an earlier stage than when the disease has taken root.

Here are six reasons you should not delay premarital counselling until closer to the wedding:

1. You need time to prepare, practice and adjust to newly gained wisdom before marriage,

2. You may realise that your relationship still needs more work before committing to

marriage and thus allowing you time to work on your relationship before marriage,

3.   You may realise you are about to marry the wrong person for you and the further you are from the wedding date, the better,

4.   You may realise your partner is reluctant to improve or labour to lay a solid foundation for a happy marriage and this may be a red flag never to ignore,

5.   To find out early, if your partner is thinking long term with you,

6.   To allow for any unforeseen delays that may delay finishing your programme before the wedding.

I once counselled a couple; they had already started with wedding plans the time they came to my office. After three sessions, I requested they postpone the wedding, as I could see clearly that their relationship's tensile strength was too weak. Usually, I see people with eyes of hope and patience, but in this case, there were so many red flags collected and ignored. Obviously, few people in love would listen to such advice. They stopped attending the sessions and the next time I heard from one of them was after they

162

had separated and called off the wedding. My intention was to buy more time for them before marriage to put their house in order. Not the separation that became inevitable the more they drew closer to the wedding.

At all times, the breakup of a relationship can never be compared to a divorce, and a relationship breakup today is easier than a relationship or marriage breakup postponed to the future. Delaying an inevitable breakup can be fatal. The longer the relationship, the harder it is to walk out of it. Just like potatoes, the more they age in your kitchen, the faster they become a source of solanine poisoning. I was empathetic to the couple that called off their wedding as they delayed too long to seek help and I believe had they knocked on my door earlier or been patient with me, they would have a better chance of succeeding to a happy marriage.

In acquiring wisdom and knowledge, timing is everything. Plan well and be on time to learn and avoid regret. It is of no use to know how to pass statistics after being expelled from school. It is less beneficial to start and learn how to have a happy marriage after the wedding. Personal experiences of failure are less favourable than learning from others. You can learn and do well in marriage without having to learn from your own failures should you choose wisdom before a time of testing.

After the vows, you cannot get premarital counselling, hence the name pre-marital. As long as you are not married, you are an excellent candidate for premarital counselling. As soon as you feel comfortable with your relationship and hope that there is potential to end in marriage, then you are ready for premarital counselling. I think six months to a year into the relationship is more than enough to find out this potential and decide to start premarital counselling. If you are not sure after a year, it is a red flag enough to quit the relationship and not waste each other's time.

Chapter 13

The who and how of premarital counselling.

After discussing the what and when of premarital counselling, we can now focus on the who and how. Finding a counsellor is easy, but finding the right and the best counsellor for your unique relationship may not be so easy. Just like searching for a great course to do, you will also need to take some time to research and find the best services available to you in the market.

If you are a faith person, I strongly recommend you find a counsellor who is of the same faith as you, as faith and religion play a critical role in marriage and family culture. Your premarital counselling should be tailored to your faith beliefs rather than going against them. Because I am a Christian, I cannot teach in my courses in support of anal sex. I cannot recommend an open relationship and on finances, I encourage biblical principles like giving and tithe.

It is hard to be trained by someone whom you disagree with in many aspects.

I recommend you find a counsellor who has a passion for marriage and has proof of successful marriages they have worked on. Passion is a great indicator of commitment and value to a person. You may just be a number to the counsellor if they lack passion, but with passion, you are more than just a dollar figure. With passion to help couples, your counsellor will easily go extra miles for your good.

Experience and wisdom are also significant factors to consider. The counsellor bears these characteristics not necessarily with age, but in the words he or she speaks and the fruits they bear. Experience is an excellent teacher, though not the best teacher. Personal experiences are impactful, though not enough to qualify or disqualify a counsellor.

I have come across a divorced marriage counsellor who has great wisdom for couples to stay married, and a counsellor who has been married for decades but has the worst marriage advice I have ever heard. Personal experiences are great for empathy and are a treasure if they can translate the experiences into great lessons for couples.

I know there are some counsellors who advise couples that fights and arguments are normal in marriage. I understand they speak sometimes from personal experiences and offer brilliant solutions on how to come back and win as a couple after a fight. In my personal experience, my wife and I have mastered the art of conflict de-escalation and negotiation, hence we can never experience an argument or fight, and I also teach how not to fight in marriage.

You cannot base your decision solely on the experiences the counsellor has, as you will not have the same experiences. Your goal is never to replicate your counsellors' experiences, but to learn from them and create your own better encounters. Do not choose a counsellor who majors on their personal experiences because they are personal. If personal experiences are from relationship principles, they are safe to advise and teach others because principles applied in different circumstances produce the same results.

One day, my wife and I were invited and in return honoured the invitation to a close friend's wedding. A certain lady had prepared a quarter hour speech. She spoke many sensible things but somehow related marriage to a boxing ring. As she was married, she narrated that the ring she was wearing was a similitude of a boxing ring. Couple's fight but never go to bed with unresolved issues. Had the newly-weds not gained wisdom before this, they probably would get their boxing gloves soon after the honeymoon. Whoever counsels you can cancel your hopes for marital happiness.

The who factor also determines the cost of the counselling services. It is best to get value for money, shop around and compare cost and quality in the same bracket. Do not compromise on quality, opting for a cheaper option. Usually, couples are working with limited resources to finance their wedding and premarital counselling simultaneously. Hence, premarital preparation may seem like a luxury. Quality things in life do not come cheap.

Some premarital counselling training sessions are cheaper because they are delivered in a class format or couples group setting. This form of premarital training is good at saving money but will yield nothing close to having an exclusive session with the counsellor. I explored the classroom format in the past, as I had many counselling requests. I could not handle all requests had I taken them exclusively (one couple per session). Within a group setting, participation from the couples was very low. After four sessions, I sent them a questionnaire to get feedback from the group of five couples and they all cited privacy concerns as they could not freely ask or give their personal accounts in the presence of other couples.

A group setting may be cheaper but will not explore every depth and length of your relationship experiences. Private sessions encourage a lot of openness, and offer solutions with high precision, yet the cost will be more than group settings. You will need to find your unique balance between cost and quality.

It is wise to not seek the services of a counsellor who is a relative or friend of your fiancé. You should not have many relationships with your counsellor other than that of a counsellor-client relationship to avoid a conflict of interest. Suppose you are a church member, and the counselling pastor is your fiancé's uncle or mother. Such a relationship may sometimes undermine the potential of counselling.

Your counsellor's education or accreditation is also a factor not to ignore. They should have attained some sort of training that shows their effort in learning and personal development towards their counselling profession. Affiliation with anybody would be great, as the counsellor is bound to operate within certain principles and the body provides oversight. Should there be wrongdoing, or you have a complaint, you will know where to report such a counsellor so that they cannot continue on a wrong path.

Ask for referrals from friends and colleagues. Usually, this is a great way to find a counsellor, as you will have a testimonial from someone whom you trust to give an honest recommendation.

The choice of who counsels you is as important as the decision to marry. A great counsellor will give your marriage a brilliant head start from normal challenges young couples are facing. Someone said, "to see far, you must stand on the shoulders of a giant". I think this is true with counselling. Your counsellor becomes the giant on whose shoulders you stand on to see far into a lifetime of marriage.

If you choose wisely on who to counsel you, you will ensure a win on the how part of counselling. Who counsels you determines how they counsel you. It is impossible to choose the how without meeting the who first. The "who" will determine the yield or return on investment you will enjoy.

Chapter 14

Premarital counselling vs. marriage counselling.

Premarital counselling is not to be confused with marriage counselling and is a unique type of counselling in its own right. The two may vary in terms of timing, their overall aim, and the way they are applied, yet each one is vitally important in its respective setting. Both forms of counselling are important. You cannot miss premarital counselling banking on marriage counselling and the opposite is true. You cannot do premarital counselling and expect it to suffice for your lifelong marriage. Taking part in premarital counselling is to get ready or qualify for marriage and marital counselling is to stay in the marriage.

The primary difference between the two counselling forms is the timing of the counselling sessions. The premarital counselling must start and finish before the vows. Post-wedding, any counselling will not be characterised as premarital. It's your responsibility to find a counsellor who offers a program you like and register for it well ahead of your wedding day.

Marriage counselling lacks a definite start and finish date as compared to premarital counselling. Owing to the fixed end date of premarital counselling, it is easy for couples to prioritise and complete the programme. It is imperative for couples to sacrifice and finish the course before the wedding day. Many married couple's desire to continue with counselling services, but because they do not have a fixed time period, they easily fall into procrastination.

When a couple takes a laid-back approach and procrastinates, there is no telling to when this can end unless they encounter trouble in marriage. As a marriage counsellor, I have grown to realise that people will seek my services only when there is trouble in paradise. Just like most people visit a medical doctor when in need of medical attention. Few people visit the doctor for preventive advice or treatments, the same is with marriage counsellors.

It will take a lot of intentionality from a married couple to schedule their counselling services as often as they wish. A lot of dedication to attend a marriage conference. A lot of willpower to buy books and read than it takes an unmarried person planning to marry.

The principal aim of premarital counselling is to educate and train you for marriage, to avoid marital problems, pre-empt and reduce the risk of divorce that emanates from a lack of preparation. Marriage counselling, however, intends to enrich marriages to reach their full potential and to solve any problems as and when they arise.

Marriage counselling is like a football coach giving tips and advising his players while playing on the pitch. Premarital counselling is all the coaching and training that happened in the training camp before the games. Before the game starts, they invest much effort into preparation. However, during the match, a player can get advice on how to play better against the opponent's tactics. As a result, if a player skips camp and training, they will be no match for the opponents. During the match, this player has pressure to learn and practise what they missed during camp training time. At the same time, teammates, cheerleaders, and fans will expect them to perform competitively.

My volleyball coach used to say, "the game is won or lost during preparation" and I found it to be true. The quality of our preparation usually gave us a competitive advantage against our opponents. The same is true for marriage. There is coaching and training many days before the ultimate game and coaching will still happen in the game, and these two are effective in their respective places.

Companies use on-the-job training as a critical capacity building tool. In marriage, you will both need coaching while being great spouses to each other. This coaching is not as intense as premarital counselling, but is critical to ensure you stay on the right path. Everyone needs a coach in life, no matter how excellent you are. I am a marriage counsellor, but I have a coach for my marriage.

The day you think you know it all and no human alive can coach you is the day your downfall begins. Having a coach and mentor is not a sign of being a troubled person, but a sign that makes a pro out of an amateur. Every pro athlete has a coach, no one can outgrow learning and mentorship. Mike Tyson had Cus D'Amato mentor him to become a world champion. Steve Jobs was a mentor to Mark Zuckerberg, and Freddie Laker mentored Richard Branson. Who is or will coach you to your greatness in marriage?

Coaching, training, and mentorship is a foundation to all greatness. Marital greatness is an achievement, something worth fighting for. Unlike in sport where masses celebrate your victories, marital greatness is something you strive for that only you and your family can celebrate the victories that masses of people will never know.

The nature of counselling sessions and content also differ between premarital counselling and marital counselling. In premarital counselling, you will dwell more on the future while in marital counselling, you dwell in the present. Premarital counselling assumes you have not experienced many aspects of marriage, while marriage counselling comes to refine past and current experiences. For example, in premarital counselling, we advise wisdom on how you will deal with your in-laws who are not present, but for marital counselling, we deal with established in-law relationships.

Marital counselling will be problem or solution-based counselling, while premarital counselling assumes the teaching and preventative form of counselling. Indeed, there is a lot of intersectionality in content and customization of the two forms of counselling, yet there are obvious differences that must be recognized and respected. As you journey in your love life, understand the importance of each counselling and such will correctly order your steps to success.

Chapter 15

Learning by books.

Readers are outstanding leaders. In case you have not realised, whether you are the wife or husband, you are both leaders of a marriage that will produce a family and lineage. Leaders read to learn, improve, gain insights, ideas, deepen problem-solving skills and sharpen their vision. If you apply the same effort to your marriage, you will never become a boring spouse.

I strongly recommend reading books on relationships, love, marriage, family, communication, sex and many other related topics. Books are a valuable source of knowledge and wisdom for your relationship or marriage. In today's world, everyone's a reader. You simply must be intentional in choosing what you read the most. Instead of reading a lot on WhatsApp, Facebook, Tweeter and many other social media sites, you can read a book for your edification.

I never knew that "I am sorry" was not apology enough until I read the book 5 Languages of apology by Dr Gary Chapman. I firmly believed that it doesn't matter how I apologise. No one should hold a grudge after I offer an apology. This was until I learned from the book that the attitude, words, feelings, and commitments are key aspects of an apology, and sometimes with restitution. This helped me to keep friendships, and I became better at mending relationships. The book is one of my five-star books in my library, part of books I do not share or lend to anyone. This is so because I strongly believe it strengthened my marriage and made my courtship days a lot easier. I became an adult with a vague knowledge of how to say sorry, and misunderstood why sorry is important. However, the book taught me that the words "I am sorry" are as important as the words "I love you" in relationships.

Only by reading this book did I learn that apologising is a sign of strength and not weakness. I read this book on apology in 2010 and I am still reaping the rewards of the knowledge I gained a decade later. That is the power of books. Another mind-altering book on marriage I read before I got married was Gary Chapman's Things I wish I'd known before we got married. The book sobered my expectations of marriage and gave me a smart mind-set for relationships.

Books are a patient teacher. You can always go back and re-learn from the book. Every book I read on relationships, I have also shared it with my wife to read. This is key to every marriage. You need to be feeding from the same source, so you learn and grow together at the same pace. If your partner is reluctant to read books, maybe they may find audio books interesting.

I listen to audiobooks while at the gym or jogging, while driving and sometimes while playing games. You should be creative with your efforts to learn from books. Should your partner not be keen to read or listen to books, I recommend you request and schedule some time to share with them all you have learned from a book. You can use this time to explain your key takeaways and lead a discussion on your newly gained wisdom.

In His wisdom, God left us with a book for us to read and meditate on, the bible. The bible has since been the best-selling book of all time across languages and nations of the world. Christianity has since prospered because of a book that communicates reality into the followers' daily lives. Only strong and devoted Christians read their bibles every day. Your strength in marriage is determined by your reading capacity.

What you read is more important than just reading. Be careful and diligently screen every book. Align yourself with authors that have the same moral beliefs and value system as yours. If you read a book that normalises fighting and arguing in relationships, you will soon expect a fight and think something is wrong when you do not argue. That is how powerful books are. Choose your books wisely. I know an author who recommends spicing up marriage by introducing a third person to your sex life. Reading such a book when you do not subscribe to such thought will cause confusion and weaken your sensitivity to that matter. The secret is in what you read.

If you read a book by an author who has been doing something for thirty years, you are absorbing all their thirty years' worth of wisdom in a few hours. Reading and learning from many books on marriage will literally make you a seasoned spouse in marriage.

Reading books will challenge your imagination and introduce new ideas. I read my first motivational book at fourteen. The book title was "It's time to unleash your greatness!" written by Milton Kamwendo. The book spoke to me like he wrote it just for me. I saw my imagination changing, started solving my teen problems, and my school grades improved until I graduated from high school. Books carry in them a capacity to alter the direction of your life.

Part C

Final remarks

The costs of a poor, unhappy, unsatisfying marriage that ends in divorce can be avoided by simply preparing well for marriage and there is no better place to do so than premarital counselling. If you love yourself and love your partner, I strongly forbid you to marry without going through a full premarital counselling program or course. Love yourself enough to pay the price now and enjoy the rewards later.

Don't make the commitment of marriage until you have the appropriate training and guidance. Don't let yourself have a mediocre marriage. Do not underestimate the significance of premarital preparation, and strive to begin your marriage correctly and at the highest level. Wisdom is profitable to direct.

If you know someone who is engaged, show them your support by giving them this book. I believe the value of this book to a couple that is intending to marry is the difference between a future troubled marriage and a happy marriage. A future divorcee and a future happy husband or wife. This book allows you an opportunity to be part of their happily ever after love story.

The choice to marry is yours, and the success or failure of the marriage will also be your responsibility. This is a hard truth, hard to tell someone who has already failed in marriage. If you practise the wisdom offered to you in this book, remember to inspire hope for others through your most certain success in marriage.

I would like to hear from you, kindly contact me on this email; muranduwalter@gmail.com.

www.ingramcontent.com/pod-product-compliance
Lightning Source LLC
Chambersburg PA
CBHW051109050726
47592CB00002B/735